HISTORY OF MOVIE COMEDY

HISTORY OF MOVIE COMEDY

Janice Anderson

This edition produced exclusively for

 **WHSMITH**

Photographic acknowledgments
Photographs from The Kobal Collection,
London,
with the following exceptions:
Frank Driggs Collection, New York, pages 7, 33,
57 bottom, 62, 85, 96, 133, 154, 155, 159, 160
top; PIC Publicity/HandMade Films, London,
page 124

Front cover: *My Little Chickadee*
                (Universal, 1940)
Back cover: *The Kid* (First National/
                Charles Chaplin Corporation,
                1921)
Frontispiece: Monty Python's *The Meaning of
                Life* (HandMade Films, 1983)

**This edition produced exclusively for
W H Smith**

Published by
Deans International Publishing
52–54 Southwark Street, London SE1 1UA
A division of The Hamlyn Publishing Group Limited
London · New York · Sydney · Toronto

Printed by Graficromo s.a., Cordoba, Spain

CONTENTS

INTRODUCTION

'Charlot', a poster by French artist Roberty, published c.1917, emphasizes Charlie Chaplin's international fame as a movie comedy star.

To paraphrase Mark Twain, man is the only animal that laughs – and needs to. We laugh at our failures and our inadequacies because laughter is better than crying – it is certainly more optimistic. And we laugh at our successes and our pleasures because laughter increases our delight in them.

The cinema has given laughter a truly universal base in our century, the medium that has enabled comedians to put their views of life before world-wide audiences. This book, in describing the various kinds of film comedy and the actors and actresses who depict it, hopes to come to some conclusion on a definition of movie comedy – not an easy task, since different people laugh at different things, without being able to tell you why. Take four different scenes in four dissimilar movies:

In *The Immigrant*, Charlie Chaplin's Tramp is in a cheap restaurant where a large bullying waiter has just thrown someone out for not having enough money to pay the bill. The Tramp, who is going to have to pay for Edna Purviance's meal as well as his own, knows that he is a penny short. What to do? The waiter, in taking another customer's money, drops a coin. With lightning speed, the Tramp's foot descends on it. The waiter has heard the sound of his foot on the floor and looks round menacingly. How can the Tramp get the coin to his table without the waiter's noticing?

In *A Day at the Races*, Chico, dressed as an ice-cream salesman selling 'tutsi-frutsi ice-cream-a', cons Groucho, who is about to place a bet, into buying a form-book that will give him the name of the winner. When Groucho looks at the book, he finds that he cannot understand it, so Chico sells him another book that will reveal the secret of the first one ... Eventually, Groucho has an armful of books, the betting window has closed, the race has been run and the horse that Groucho fancied in the first place has been declared the winner.

In *Les Vacances de Monsieur Hulot* (*Monsieur Hulot's Holiday*), M. Hulot

(Jacques Tati) is sitting on the beach doing a painting. The tide comes in and the mug into which M. Hulot has been dipping his brush floats off. He does not notice, and every time he reaches out to the mug with his brush, the tide obligingly brings it back to exactly the right place.

In *Cet Obscur Objet du Désir* (*That Obscure Object of Desire*), Fernando Rey thinks that, at last, the girl he desires and who has been rejecting him despite everything he does for her is going to give in.

He approaches her – and discovers a corset as impregnable as a suit of armour.

Not everyone would laugh at each of these scenes, for everyone's sense of the comic is different. Yet, we can see that each is funny, offering an amusing comment on life, and we can see that its humour comes from the relationships between people and between people and objects.

As pieces of movie comedy, the scenes also have in common a strong element of

Harold Lloyd's most memorable scene, the clock-hanging act, was the high spot of the silent comedy, Safety Last *(Pathé/Hal Roach, 1923).*

7

Right: Ollie has copped it again, this time in Saps at Sea, *one of Laurel and Hardy's later feature films made for Hal Roach (United Artists/ Hal Roach, 1940).*

Opposite: Stylish poster for Ernst Lubitsch's deliciously witty comedy That Uncertain Feeling *(United Artists, 1941).*

Below: All four Marx Brothers were featured in Animal Crackers, *the film version of their Broadway hit show (Paramount, 1930).*

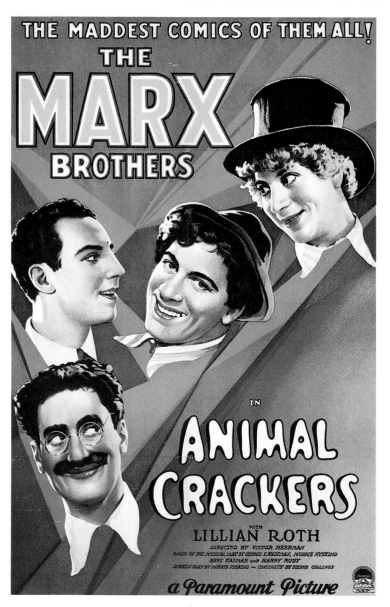

suspense and a fine sense of timing. The suspense inherent in the scenes holds our attention throughout. Is the Tramp going to get that coin? Is Groucho really going to be had for a sucker again? When will the tide stop bringing the mug back to the right spot? Will Fernando Rey achieve fulfilment this time?

Timing is that sixth sense that enables an action, a gesture, even a look to be performed at exactly the right moment to make the viewer laugh, even though he or she may have seen the joke coming. In the days of the silent movie, timing was a matter of movement and expression, and often of movement alone. With the talkies, it also became an essential element in getting the spoken word across.

Bob Hope is a master of timing, as was Groucho Marx, who could combine funny movements with words in such a way that even quite inane pieces of dialogue would produce roars of laughter. Remember the scene in *A Night at the Opera* where he is entertaining Margaret Dumont in his private hotel-room? As they sit down, they engage in a ridiculous back-and-forth series of thank-yous.

But if timing is important, even more so is a belief in the seriousness of what you are doing. The really great film comics have all taken a considerable interest in the screenplays of their films, knowing that without a good script there cannot be a great performance. Some, such as Chaplin and Woody Allen, have written their

SOL LESSER
presents

MERLE OBERON · Melvyn DOUGLAS

Ernst Lubitsch's

THAT UNCERTAIN FEELING

with **BURGESS MEREDITH** and ALAN MOWBRAY · HARRY DAVENPORT · EVE ARDEN · SIG RUMANN

Produced and directed by ERNST LUBITSCH

Screenplay by DONALD OGDEN STEWART · Adaptation by WALTER REISCH · *Released thru* UNITED ARTISTS

Above: How Monsieur Hulot crosses a busy street, as demonstrated by Jacques Tati in Park Lane in London, where the French film-maker had come to promote Mon Oncle *in 1958.*

Opposite: Professor Julius Kelp, alias Jerry Lewis, inventing the potion that will turn him into the suave, sexy, confident Buddy Love in The Nutty Professor *(Paramount, 1963).*

own. Abbott and Costello left the writing to others, and were not too concerned with who those others were; the result was that the lack of a good writer in the background showed in too many of the duo's later films.

And, distinct from the merely funny comedian, the really great movie comic simply *is*. He is not trying to be funny. Jack Lemmon, whether in *The Apartment*, *Some Like It Hot* or *Avanti!*, gives totally serious protrayals of men caught in the tangles of fate. Jerry Lewis, as *The Nutty Professor* or anything else, is always *trying* to be funny. Lemmon is a great comic, Lewis is a funny man – and sometimes not very funny.

It is a truism of the movie business that if, on a film set, everyone is giggling at their own jokes, hugging themselves with glee at the hilarity of what they have been doing, then that film is going to be a turkey. Comedy is a damn serious business.

There have, of course, been many funny films, and long may there continue to be so, but great comedy is rather rarer. More than just a tickling of the public's fancy, it is a lightening of the dark places in men's souls, a noting of the fact that human nature is perhaps more misled, more ignorant or just plain lost than intentionally evil. Great comedy gives a glimmer of hope for the future of the human race.

It is perhaps a recognition of this that has prompted the American Academy of Motion Picture Arts and Sciences to give so many special awards to makers of comedy films – more than to, say, makers of westerns or thrillers. In the early days of the Oscar ceremonies, there used to be an Oscar for Best Comedy – Laurel and Hardy won the first one in 1931/2 for *The Music Box* – and was, in essence, an Oscar for shorts, discontinued in 1935. Numerous comedies have won major awards since then, including Best Picture,

Woody Allen, glasses firmly in place, fights for the Czar in Love and Death *(United Artists/Jack Rollins–Charles H. Joffe, 1975).*

Best Director, Best Actor/Actress, but the special awards list is rather more than just a few names; it is a roll-call of some of the greatest names in movie comedy, including Charlie Chaplin, Mack Sennett, Buster Keaton, Harold Lloyd, Ernst Lubitsch, Stan Laurel, Groucho Marx, Bob Hope and Danny Kaye, and others who have been serious as well as comedy actors, such as Alec Guinness and Cary Grant.

They are all here in this book, displaying their 'distinguished contributions to the art of the motion picture', to quote Ernst Lubitsch's special award citation. Of course, there are many others who are not here because it would take an encyclopedia to acknowledge all the talented people who have given so much to audiences through the medium of comedy.

LEAVE 'EM LAUGHING:
MOVIE COMEDY'S EARLY DAYS

Historians of the cinema usually cite a brief piece of film, *Fred Ott's Sneeze*, as the first movie comedy. This seminal work was probably shot at Thomas Edison's picture studio – the first to be custom-built for making movies – at East Orange, New Jersey in 1893, though it may have been made earlier.

Fred Ott was one of Thomas Edison's assistants, and Edison was, of course, the great pioneer of moving picture photography who had invented the Kinetoscope in 1889. In this, the images on lengths of film revolving on spools were projected on to the end of a cabinet with the help of an electric light. By dropping a coin through a slot, the machine was turned on and one viewer at a time was able to squint through the peephole at the fifty feet of film that lasted a minute. Edison began selling his Kinetoscope in commercial numbers, and in American cities from coast to coast, whole 'parlours' lined with the machines were given over to its use. Each cost only a penny to operate, and the young and the poor flocked in.

However, the tiny peephole view into the cabinet was obviously unsatisfactory,

How our great-grandparents viewed moving pictures, as illustrated in a brochure for the French 'Compagnie génerale des Phonographes, Cinématographes et appareils de Précision'.

Right: Lights, camera, action as a scene is shot in Thomas Edison's studio in The Bronx, New York, sometime before the First World War.

Opposite: Programme for a variety evening which included short films at London's Royal Theatre of Varieties, Holborn, in 1898.

Below: This poster for the 'Cinématographe Lumière' shows the audience laughing at one of the Lumière brothers' earliest films, L'Arroseur arrosé (1895).

and by the mid-1890s, films were being projected on to screens. In February 1896, the brothers Louis and Auguste Lumière gave a public performance of their Ciné-matographe at a hall in central London. The film, made in 1895 and already shown to audiences in France, included views of the French city of Lyon, the mailboat from France arriving at Folke-stone, and a short comic piece called *L'Arroseur arrosé* ('Teasing the Gar-dener'). In it, a man is shown at work in a garden, watering plants; a boy sneaks up, puts his foot on the hose and the flow of water stops; the gardener, surprised, looks at the end of the hose – and receives a faceful of water when the boy lifts his foot. *Fred Ott's Sneeze* had simply been an amusing act filmed as it happened; the Lumières' film was an artificial comic situation, with a beginning, a middle and an end, in which the comic consequences of various actions were played out, the main one being, of course, that the audience laughed. All early films, even if only of a lion in his cage in a zoo, were entertaining because they were a novelty, but a comedy involved extra participation by the audience: laughter.

Comedy proved to be international, too, for the Lumières' gardener film found its way across the Atlantic as well as the Channel. The moving-picture projector, afterwards called the Vitascope, which Thomas Armat first developed, and which was manufactured by the Edison Com-pany and, in its early stages, used Edison's Kinetoscope films, was in operation at Koster and Bial's Music Hall in New York by 1896, billed as 'Thomas Edison's latest marvel'. On the programme, along with such items as *Kaiser Wilhelm Reviewing His Troops*, *Venice with Gondolas*, *Sea Waves* and *Butterfly Dance* were two Lumière films, *Mammy Washing Her Child* and *L'Arroseur arrosé*.

Until the turn of the century, moving pictures remained, at best, very much an item on the bills of music halls or vaude-ville houses, usually the closing act. There were plenty of 'news' items – Bert Ber-nard's film of Queen Victoria's Diamond Jubilee procession in 1897 was shown at London's famous Alhambra theatre for five months – and, particularly in Britain, plenty of short comic turns, many of them actually filmed on the Alhambra's flat roof and using the theatre's scenery. The

A 'blind' man with an eye for a shapely leg: a wryly humorous moment from an early Biograph short.

films were made at the instigation of Robert W. Paul, the manager of the Alhambra, who was always on the look-out for novelties to keep audiences in his theatre and out of those of his rivals. One of Paul's early successes, made in 1896, was called *The Soldier's Courtship*. The plot was fairly basic: a soldier and his girlfriend courting on a park bench: an old lady sits down and gradually edges the couple off the bench; they stand up suddenly, the bench tips up and the old lady hits the ground hard, the bench ending up on top of her. Big laugh from the audience.

This was also the year in which the American Mutoscope and Biograph Company, which was to play such a large part in silent film production in the United States, was formed. The company, set up by former associates of Thomas Edison, was his first big rival and used machines and projectors just dissimilar enough from Edison's to get round his patents. One of their most famous early films caused audiences to shout with fear, not laughter, since it depicted a train apparently coming straight out of the screen at sixty miles an hour. In 1896, the Vitagraph Company was formed, while in France, the bearers of such famous names as Méliès, Gaumont and Pathé were all well into the movie-making business.

It was George Méliès who did more than anyone to get the moving picture off the end of the music-hall programme and into its own picture theatre. Méliès was a magician and illusionist, who very quickly saw how the moving picture could be used to create the greatest illusions of all. He made hundreds of short 'magical mystery' films around 1900, and these were shown all over Europe and America, their ideas being quickly copied by other filmmakers. *A Trip to the Moon*, the first film to be truly a narrative, appeared in 1902. Complete with rockets and moonscapes, *A Trip to the Moon* was splendid science fiction, as was Méliès' 1904 *An Impossible Voyage*.

Méliès films were not just full of clever tricks to show off an illusionist's genius, though the way he used the camera to play jokes on his audience was an essential part of his comedy. His films also had genuinely comic elements in them, for he was not averse to satirizing the pretensions of over-confident scientists, professors and the like. He also made great use of those vaudeville stand-bys, tumblers, acrobats, contortionists and gymnasts, whose astonishing physical power could be turned into comic pranks.

The year of *A Trip to the Moon* was also the year in which the first motion picture theatre, called The Electric, opened in Los Angeles. Britain's first continuous film theatre, called the Daily Bioscope, opened in London in 1906, and the newspaper announcement of this important event included a piece of verse that emphasized the place comedy would have in the enterprise:

To the world the world we show,
We make the world to laugh,
And teach each hemisphere to know
How lives the other half.

This verse was signed 'Elge'. Elge? The name came from the initials of Léon Gaumont, the pioneer French movie man who had set up the Gaumont Film Company in London in 1898. This company began to make films in England the following year.

According to film historian John Montgomery, Gaumont's first film player was a London costermonger called Mike Savage who appeared in the firm's earliest comedy *The Fisherman's Mishap*. Many of their players were, in fact, music-hall artists during these early days, including that great Scotsman, Harry Lauder.

Gaumont's films, which were shot all over the world, quickly began to sell internationally, including hundreds to America. A considerable amount of comedy shown in American movie houses at this time was coming from Europe where, in France, Germany, Italy, the Scandinavian countries and Britain, comedy films were being produced in great quantity. Language was no barrier, of course, since there were no spoken words needing translation, and American audiences' demand for films was such that exhibitors could use all they could get from any source.

Some of what they got was very imaginative indeed. Take the work of two British pioneers, James Williamson and George A. Smith. These two men worked in the rather unlikely ambience of the

This picture well demonstrates the attention to detail which helped George Méliès achieve the amazing effects of his films. This wrecked railway carriage featured in An Impossible Voyage *(1904).*

Above: In the motion picture theatres of the Nickelodeon age they would flash a notice on the screen saying 'Ladies! Kindly Remove Your Hats'. These potential customers for Poli's in Waterbury, Connecticut, wear the reason why.

Opposite: The man in the silk topper was Max Linder, the always elegant, always in trouble Frenchman who achieved international screen popularity before the First World War.

quiet seaside resort of Hove, on England's south coast. Scottish-born Williamson used what were, for his period, quite sophisticated techniques, his *Attack on a China Mission Station* (1900), for instance, including cross-cutting and parallel action techniques. Comedies made at the studio he built in Hove included *Why the Wedding Was Put Off* and *Two Naughty Boys Upsetting the Spoons* (both 1898) and the surrealistic *The Clown Barber* (1899) in which a barber cut off his customer's head, shaved it, then put it back on the customer. George Smith built his own movie camera in the mid-1890s and later patented Kinemacolor, the first commercially successful colour film technique. His films made great use of the special, or trick, effect in which he was to prove as innovative as Méliès. On the stage that he had built in a public park in Hove, Smith produced comic films by the hundred from about 1899 until after the First World War.

Then there were the Italians and the French, whose films crossed international boundaries with scarcely a flicker to indicate to the largely working-class and also heavily immigrant audiences of American cities that they were being entertained by comic actors and actresses whose native tongue certainly was not English.

Many French film players were experienced stage clowns and comedians, who performed in George Méliès' clever tricks to good effect, but one rather different actor was Gabriel-Maximilien Leuvielle who came to films via the legitimate stage, having started his acting career as a teenager in Bordeaux. He moved to Paris in 1904 and, within a year, was acting both on the stage and in Pathé films. Since films were very much a *déclassé* profession, and probably harmful to a budding actor's career, Leuvielle thought up the pseudonym Max Linder for his film *persona*. By 1910 it was film actor Max Linder, not stage actor Gabriel-Maximilien, who was

L'HOMME AU CHAPEAU
DE SOIE

MAX LINDER

an international celebrity, having become via his films one of the most popular of all comedians before the First World War.

Linder wrote and directed most of his own films, in which he usually figured as a very dapper, exquisitely turned-out gentleman in immaculate tails, top hat, white gloves, spats and so on. He was a genuine dandy, not someone aspiring to such a position as was Charlie Chaplin's Tramp, and was also a handsome man, which set him apart from the usual run of film comics. Linder's comedy – marked by his great ingenuity in dreaming up gags and funny stories, rather than by any great skill in playing to the camera or in developing character – arose from the sight of this dandy attempting quite seriously to do things – ice skate, box, fight duels, make pancakes, drive recalcitrant motor cars – that would inevitably end

with his ego being sadly dented and in need of a dust down.

The First World War wrecked Linder's career. Serving as a soldier, he was wounded after months in the trenches, and eventually he had a mental breakdown. Although he returned to film-making in France, he could not recapture his old popularity and so he went to the United States at the invitation of the Essanay studio, who were looking for a replacement for Charlie Chaplin. (Ironically, Chaplin was later to say that Linder had been one of the great influences on his early career.) Illness forced Linder back to Europe, and it was not until 1921 that he returned to the States, where among the three films he made was a still-celebrated parody of Douglas Fairbank's *The Three Musketeers*, called *The Three Must-Get-Theres* (1922), and the film that many

Max Linder struggling out of a difficult position in his fine American-made feature Seven Years' Bad Luck *(Robertson-Cole, 1921).*

consider his best, *Seven Years' Bad Luck* (1921), basically a series of unrelated, awful incidents that befell Max as a consequence of breaking a mirror. The gags were very funny and wonderfully ingenious.

But success was to elude Max Linder and he returned to Europe where, depressed and ill, he committed suicide in 1925. His wife, who had made a suicide pact with him, died alongside him.

Other Frenchmen besides Max Linder made the leap to international recognition before the First World War. Many of them, though, were quite anonymous: it was the characters they played that audiences came to know, rather than the actors themselves. And, since there was nothing in the films to indicate the names of the actors or the characters they played, the latter's names could be changed to suit local audiences. Thus, the French knockabout comedian, André Deed, was known to audiences in France as 'Boireau' or 'Gribouille', to the Italians as 'Cretinetti', to the Spanish as 'Torribo' or 'Sanchez' and to the English-speaking world as 'Foolshead' or 'Jim'. The French Gaumont company's dwarf Bout-de-Zan was renamed 'Tiny Tim' in England where his films were very successful, and Charles Prince, another French comedian, who worked in the Pathé comedies, was called 'Rigadin' in France, 'Wiffles' in Britain, and 'Tarfutini' in Italy. As late as the early Twenties, the enormously popular Hollywood comedian, Larry Semon – who appeared in many one- and two-reelers for Vitagraph from 1917, often in whiteface and wearing outsize trousers held up with shoulder straps – was called 'Zigoto' in France, 'Rindolini' in Italy and

Larry Semon still wears the traditional white make-up of the clown in The Hunter.

'Romasin' in Spain, the names suggesting that Semon was seen as being part of the centuries-old tradition of the *Commedia dell'arte* clown, rather than as the purveyor of a new kind of comedy.

It should not be thought that because all these Europeans found easy niches in the movie houses of the United States there was not much comedy coming from American companies. Indeed, they had been making jokes for the screen from the earliest days. The Edison company's *Washday Trouble* of *c.* 1895 was a variation of the boy-hose-water theme, though this time it was a tub of water that the boy tipped over a woman trying to do her laundry, and *Trouble in a Chinese Laundry* (did someone at Edison have a laundry fixation?) was a frenetically active chase involving a policeman among the washtubs.

For a long time, though, these comedy films were just short jokes — less than a minute — that made no effort to make any inter-relation between the figures acting out the joke and the joke itself. And, since they were so short, each film told just one joke: sitting through a programme of them must have been rather like reading those bumper joke books so popular with kids today — after a while, the jokes begin to pall.

Even after Méliès' *Trip to the Moon* pointed the way, it was some time before comedy film-makers showed the same sense of narrative — or felt any need for it — unlike the men working with more dramatic subjects whose treatments quickly followed the way signposted so graphically by Edwin S. Porter's *Life of an American Fireman* and *The Great Train Robbery*, both of which appeared in 1903.

True, American comedy films were, early in the new century, putting the names of the characters into the titles — 'Uncle Josh' turned up several times, as did 'Foxy Grandpa' and 'Buster Brown' — but they were given no individual personalities or real characteristics with which to bring any humanity to the jokes and japes they were acting out in front of the usually static camera.

Vitagraph, one of the most go-ahead of the early production companies that set the fledgling movie industry on its feet, had a highly popular comedy star who *did* bring real character to his parts: the gruff, rotund John Bunny, an English-born vaudeville actor who was forty-seven when he took to film-making in 1910. Bunny's comedies were usually set firmly in the domestic and working life of the average proletarian American male, one saddled with a tight-lipped, sharp-nosed, flat-chested, overly moralistic wife who disapproved of cards and gambling, drinks with the boys, pretty secretaries and just about everything that made life tolerable for a man. Bunny and the homely-looking Flora Finch, a fine comedy actress, made something like 200 shorts together on these lines, churning them out almost up to Bunny's untimely death from Bright's disease in 1915.

While the Biograph Company was still churning out quickie movie jokes and knockabout romps on one lot of sets, D. W. Griffith, employed by the same company, was elsewhere making a series of one-reel films in which he was experimenting with ways of handling real storylines that involved thought-provoking ideas requiring some sort of emotional response from audiences. Griffith also began to move the film-making process away from its static dependence on the acting style of the live theatre, throwing aside the proscenium arch with which many movie-makers were still mentally framing their scenes.

Among the supporting players working in D. W. Griffith's film was a young man who had gravitated to Biograph from the chorus of numerous Broadway musicals. His name was Mack Sennett, born Michael Sinnott, the gregarious and cheerful son of Irish immigrants. While quite quickly working his way up from supporting player to star in many of Griffith's films between 1908 and 1911, playing opposite such delightful ladies as the 'Biograph Girl' Florence Lawrence, Mary Pickford, Mabel Normand and Blanche Sweet, Sennett was also learning a great deal about the mechanics and techniques of film-making. He wrote several scripts for Griffith, kept a close watch on the director's great cameraman and collaborator Billy Bitzer, and involved himself in the business of editing and cutting films.

After a couple of years of this, Sennett, never much of an actor, had become good film-maker material with a yen for making comedies — which was a good thing

since Griffith himself never showed any great interest in the potential of comedy. By late 1910, Biograph started giving Sennett films to direct. One of the first of these was a comedy called *Comrades*; as with others he directed in 1911, he also acted in the film, in which a tramp found himself briefly enjoying the life of 'high' society, the denizens of which were seen to be unlikable hypocrites. Within a year, Sennett was in charge of most of Biograph's comedy output, at which point he left the company to set up on his own, taking with him several Biograph actors, including Fred Mace, Ford Sterling and Mabel Normand.

Mabel Normand was to become the greatest comedienne of the silent film. The daughter of a vaudeville pianist, she was just sixteen when she joined the Biograph Company in New York in 1910. After a brief period with Vitagraph she was back with Biograph late in 1911 where, directed mostly by Mack Sennett, with whom she developed a close personal relationship that lasted several years (they talked about marriage, but never made it to the altar), she grew into a talented, deliciously attractive comedienne with an instinctive sense of timing.

She moved to Sennett's own company where she starred in many of his slapstick

Mack Sennett casts a cool directorial eye over a scene full of Eastern promise for one of his silent comedy shorts.

23

Mabel Normand in peril in Barney Oldfield's Race for Life, *a Mack Sennett short made in 1913. Wielding the mallet is Ford Sterling, while Mack Sennett, on the right, tightens the chains.*

comedies, able to throw custard pies, wrestle with a baddie or pose in a bathing suit with the best of them. In *The Water Nymph* of 1912, for instance, the shapely Mabel, clad in clinging, neck-to-ankle bathing suit, high-dived into the ocean. 'The beautiful diving Venus' the Keystone poster called her, naming her as one of 'a quartet of popular fun makers', the other funsters being Sennett, Mace and Sterling. *The Water Nymph* and *Cohen Collects a Debt* were the first of Sennett's company's films, released in September 1912.

Mabel wanted to do more than throw custard pies in one- and two-reelers, however, and she began taking a hand in directing films. She directed or co-directed quite a number, including several – such as *Caught in a Cabaret, Mabel's Busy Day* and *Mabel's New Job*, all made in 1914 – with Charlie Chaplin.

It was the great success of the six-reel *Tillie's Punctured Romance*, also made in 1914, in which Mabel starred with Chaplin

and Marie Dressler, that prompted her to ask Sennett for more feature film parts. As a result, he and his financial associates, Bauman and Kessel, set up a company for her, the Mabel Normand Feature Film Company. She gave a fine performance in *Mickey*, the first film under this new deal, but Sennett, who had produced but not directed it, held it back for over a year, partly, it is said, because he could not get an exhibitor for a film that apparently departed from Mabel's popular custard-pie style. This so incensed Mabel that she decided to move to Metro, before the film, eventually released in 1918, was a hit.

Without Sennett, Mabel seemed to lose her way in Hollywood's fast-moving social whirl. Two men with whom she was linked were murdered in circumstances that dragged her into the subsequent scandals; she was rumoured to be heavily into drugs; and her confidence and her career foundered. She did make more feature films, including several with

Sennett, but after the last one in 1923, there came only a series of Hal Roach comedy shorts. The woman whom Sennett had once described as being 'as beautiful as a spring morning' died of tuberculosis and pneumonia in 1930.

'Keystone' was the name of the production company of which Mabel Normand was to be such a luminary, formed in 1912 by Sennett, with two bookies-turned-film-producers called Charles Bauman and Adam Kessel putting up the money. Over the next three years or so, this name would become synonymous with that wonderfully frenzied breed of film comedy known as slapstick. (The term was born in the world of theatre burlesque where, to encourage audiences to laugh, a prop called a 'slapstick' was used to make a slapping sound every time the comic on stage told a joke.)

Sennett directed many of the Keystone comedies and kept a tight rein on the rest, especially in the cutting-room where he was a brilliant film editor. Thus, his own quick-fire way of working, which involved keeping his actors and the story always on the move, and his attention to the details of gags and funny 'business' in his work, much of which was pure improvisation thought up in the course of the day's work, were the major influences on all Keystone's comedy. He worked out-of-doors a good deal, too, which added to the spontaneity of much of the fun, and gave a much broader, more spacious feel to his films than set-bound studio filming could achieve, and of course, the company's move west to Los Angeles made outdoor filming that much easier.

The overwhelming impression made by the archetypal Keystone film is one of

The Keystone Kops, a team of wildly absurd policemen whose gags were brilliantly inventive, were a favourite feature of Sennett comedies. Prominent in this picture are Mack Swain (centre) and Roscoe Arbuckle (right).

*Roscoe 'Fatty'
Arbuckle and Mabel
Normand teamed up
for a series of very
popular Mack Sennett
shorts about married
life, made at Keystone
in 1915–16. Here,
Mabel nearly throttles
Fatty with his bow tie.*

bald, wildly over-moustachioed. Hence the huge Roscoe 'Fatty' Arbuckle and Mack Swain, cross-eyed Ben Turpin, pop-eyed and goatee-bearded Ford Sterling, walrus-moustached Chester Conklin and Billy Bevan, and the skinny and hollow-cheeked Slim Summerville. Mabel Normand, as we have seen, found all this limiting and began to hanker for better roles in classier films, while Charlie Chaplin did not stay very long with Keystone, finding that Sennett's view of comedy allowed him little room to develop character. (Even so, Chaplin was with Sennett long enough to learn a great deal about film-making and to become one of Keystone's greatest comics.)

Sennett steered clear of pursuing moral issues in his films, though he was always ready to take the stuffing out of stuffed shirts, to lambast pretension and to knock authority in its many guises. Nor did he explore social problems or try to sort out the world's troubles, as Chaplain wanted to do. Instead, he gave the world bevies of bathing beauties and hordes of Keystone Kops so that the world could laugh.

Keystone survived as a separate company only until 1915 when, now a film company of considerable size with hordes of actors, directors, writers and gag-men on the payroll, it merged into the Triangle Film Corporation, along with two other great film-makers, Thomas Ince and D. W. Griffith.

From this period, the style of Sennett's comedies changed. The loony slapstick was still well in evidence in such films as *The Surf Girl* (1916) and in early examples in the lengthy series of 'Mabel and Fatty' films, starring Normand and Arbuckle, such as *Mabel and Fatty's Simple Life*, and *Mabel and Fatty's Married Life*, and *Miss Fatty's Seaside Lovers* (all made in 1915), the latter with Arbuckle gloriously, hugely splendid in drag. But the knock-about comedy tended to fade in the Triangle period in favour of films that looked more 'classy' and were made from properly mapped-out scripts and shooting plans. They got bigger, but not necessarily better.

Sennett had already indicated his move in this direction back in 1914 with *Tillie's Punctured Romance*, a feature-length film adapted from a stage success recently enjoyed by larger-than-life Broadway comedienne Marie Dressler, who had,

constant, frenetic movement, with people, generally photographed in long shot, moving about like breathless zany puppets, often in terrible conflict with machines: cars, boats, aeroplanes, fire engines, police vans.... These marionettes were manipulated, not by strings, but by a camera doing all sorts of tricks in the hands of a master technician.

Sennett was not too concerned about photographing his actors in close-up to allow their characters to emerge, or to give emotions time to develop. In fact, he was more interested in types than in character: he wanted to have about him people who were outrageously fat or skinny, knock-kneed, cross-eyed, ludicrously

Exuberant Marie Dressler goes for over-kill, with a hat not much smaller than her parasol in this early publicity picture.

Opposite: Douglas
Fairbanks, comedian,
maintains a
nonchalant pose in
Wild and Woolly
(Paramount–Artcraft/
Douglas Fairbanks
Film Corporation,
1917).

many years before, given Sennett his introduction to Broadway. Dressler starred in the film version with Chaplin and Normand, and most of the Keystone regulars had parts in it too, including Mack Swain, Chester Conklin, Minta Durfee (Arbuckle's wife), Phyllis Allen, Hank Mann and the Keystone Kops. The film, a story about a couple of city types (Chaplin and Normand) trying to get their hands on the money of an innocent country girl (Dressler), enjoyed no little success at the time.

The Triangle company lasted only a couple of years, Griffith pulling out in 1917, and Ince and Sennett following not long after. This was also the year in which Roscoe 'Fatty' Arbuckle – who had joined Keystone in 1913 and soon became a hugely popular star as well as a great Hollywood personality – also left to set up his own production company. As a writer and director of comedy films, he was just as successful, and was the man who gave Buster Keaton his start. Within four years, however, Arbuckle's career had been destroyed by dreadful scandal: he was accused of manslaughter over the death of a starlet, Virginia Rappe, after a party at which Arbuckle was alleged to have sexually assaulted her. Although he was eventually (after three court trials) found not guilty, he was finished in the movies.

There could be no greater contrast to the fat, baby-faced yet surprisingly athletic Arbuckle than the handsome, physically splendid Douglas Fairbanks, apparently made by nature to be the romantic hero of such films as *The Three Musketeers* (1921), *The Thief of Bagdad* (1924) and *The Black Pirate* (1926). Yet years before he made these, and at much the same time as Fatty Arbuckle, Fairbanks had been enormously successful as a comedy star.

He had the typical silent comedians' trait of being physically energetic and wonderfully clever with his body, with the added bonus that he was able to perform his incredible, apparently effortless feats with stylish grace. Whether swinging from roof beams, leaping from cliffs or horses, vaulting over furniture or rooftops, Fairbanks looked superb. He also had some excellent scripts, most of them written by Anita Loos, directed by her husband John Emerson and photographed by Victor

Fleming – a richly talented team by any standards – who worked within Fairbanks' own production companies.

Many of their films, while telling an amusing story in their own right, parodied the popular film genres of the day. *Wild and Woolly* (1917) and *The Molycoddle* (1920) joked at the expense of westerns, *The Mystery of the Leaping Fish* (1916) detective stories, and *His Majesty the*

American (1919) the *mittel*-European romance/spy story, though the latter film fired its shots more widely, to laugh at Americans' misplaced admiration for anyone with a title.

After Triangle, Sennett set up his own company, making films for release under the banner of, firstly, Adolph Zukor's Paramount, then Associate Producers and First National. He carried on with the by-now traditional two-reeler comedy film, mostly in the capacity of producer, and also branched out into feature films. The fading Mabel Normand starred in several of these, including *Molly O'* (1921) and *Oh Mabel Behave* (1922).

During the Twenties, the Sennett company, in association now with Pathé, became the umbrella under which comedy stars such as Ben Turpin, Harry Langdon

Opposite: Fun in a bakery for the cross-eyed Ben Turpin in a Sennett short, Love and Doughnuts *(Associated First National, 1921).*

and Billy Bevan were able to create their own films, with their own writing and production teams.

Ben Turpin, he of the wildly crossed eyes (insured against uncrossing with Lloyds of London) and strange rectangular moustache, had been around for years, having joined Essanay in Chicago in 1907, but did not make much of an impact until he came under Sennett's wing in 1917, when he became an extremely athletic Keystone Kop. He hit the jackpot in the 1920s with his mad parodies of some of the great male stars of his time. *The Shreik of Araby* (1923) lampooned Rudolph Valentino whose smouldering *Sheik* had made women swoon in cinema aisles in 1921; Erich von Stroheim, the bull-necked Prussian actor and director of the sensationally sophisticated and witty

Foolish Wives (1922), was cut down to size in *Three Foolish Weeks* (1924); and *The Reel Virginian* (1924) parodied William S. Hart, Tom Mix and the already well-established movie myth of the western, as exemplified by *The Virginian* which had already been made twice, in 1914 with Dustin Farnum and in 1923 by B. P. Schulberg's Preferred Pictures.

Harry Langdon was 'discovered' by Sennett in 1923 when he had a modestly successful vaudeville act involving his wife and a car. He had made a few two-reelers, none of them up to much, yet within two years of being taken on by the Sennett production team, he was just about as world-famous as the three great men of silent comedy, Chaplin, Keaton and Lloyd. The character the studio had devised for Langdon was that of a white-

Right: Harry Langdon appearing as incompetent as ever in this scene from one of the sound shorts he made for Hal Roach in 1929–30.

Lupino Lane in one of his last films, Lambeth Walk *(Me and My Gal in US). Lane was at his most popular in Hollywood in the 1920s (Capad, 1939).*

faced, babyish innocent abroad, a man inept in his dealings with everything in life, including women, who came through adversity because of his child-like, even infantile trust in the essential goodness of the world.

However, by the end of the Twenties, while the Big Three still had plenty of life left in their careers, Langdon was, to all intents and purposes, finished. It was partly a question of hubris. In the beginning, working closely with some of Sennett's best men, especially the young Frank Capra and the director Harry Edwards, Langdon became very successful in Sennett two-reelers.

In 1926, when he moved to Warner Bros., Langdon very sensibly persuaded Edwards and Capra to go with him. There, the two men created for Langdon his best, and most successful, near-feature-length films – *Tramp Tramp Tramp* in which Joan Crawford played opposite Langdon in this tale of a shoe factory, *The Strong Man* (both released in 1926) and *Long Pants* (1927). Unfortunately the naïve and not very bright Langdon thought that his success was entirely of his own making, rid himself of Capra and Edwards and launched out on his own. It was not that his solo films were all that

bad; it was only that they were not quite so good, just when his style no longer suited the times. Sound came to films too, which did not help an actor whose style was almost that of a mime artist, and his career went into a long decline, ending with his death in 1944.

Billy Bevan was different. He was a two-reeler slapstick man and, as such, was very successful, carrying his great walrus moustache like a flag through some seventy movies made for Mack Sennett in the 1920s. Most of them pushed the archetypal Sennett visual gags and exhausting chase sequences to maniac extremes, though their fantastic tricks with cars, aeroplanes, circus animals and the like meant that they had to be much more carefully plotted than in the early Sennett shorts, when improvisation had been the keynote. Australian-born Bevan was to enjoy a revival as a character actor, specializing in Cockneys in such films of the Thirties as *Cavalcade* (1933) and *The Lost Patrol* (1934), and later *Cluny Brown* (1946).

Sennett was not the only big comedy producer of the 1920s. Hundreds and thousands of comedy films poured out of the great Hollywood companies – if Paramount had its Wallace Beery and Raymond

Hatton comedies, then MGM had to have films featuring the British music-hall comedian George K. Arthur and his sidekick Karl Dane (who later had to take up carpentering on the MGM lot) – and from small, long-since forgotten studios with names like Sunshine Comedies or Campbells Comedies, or the better-remembered Educational Pictures, three of whose big names were Lupino Lane (from an English theatrical family that could trace its on-stage activities back to the time of the Stuarts), Lloyd Hamilton and Larry Semon.

Sennett's major competitor was Hal Roach, once a bit player at Universal where he had met up with and saw the potential in another bit player called Harold Lloyd. When Roach set up on his own, Lloyd was his first really successful player.

Roach's comedy output placed much more emphasis on structure and a formal plot than did Sennett's visual-gag style of picture. There were plenty of gags in Roach's films, often as frenzied and loony as anything Sennett could show, but they were generally given longer to develop, and each film had a properly constructed beginning, middle and end. The effect was of generally smoother productions, to which the increasingly sophisticated cinema audiences responded happily.

While Harold Lloyd was the greatest of Roach's early stars, there were others, carefully nurtured by Roach with his sure instinct for changing fashions and trends, who made the transition from silence to sound at the end of the Twenties. Will Rogers, Charlie (also Charley) Chase, Laurel and Hardy, Edgar Kennedy and the Our Gang kids were all part of Hal Roach's galaxy of talent.

Roach's stars were generally allowed to be real people rather than two-dimensional gag portrayers. The Our Gang kids were true children, treated with gentle, affectionate humour. Will Rogers was obviously a genuinely warm-hearted man, physically very capable of performing himself the western riding, cattle-roping and bronco-busting tricks he burlesqued in his film impersonations of the real western stars. Charlie Chase, inheritor of Harold Lloyd's place at the top of the Roach tree, was the typical American man, *genus* domestic. He usually had a name – Jimmy Jump – a wife, kids, a job, a comfortable house, and he wanted to enjoy all this in peace, not to be constantly maddened and exasperated by the vicissitudes of life, such as the troubles that beset his car (*All Wet*, 1924) or the hiccups that attacked first his small daughter at the table then himself at the movies (*Movie Night*, 1929).

Charlie Chase (centre) can't believe his eyes in Crazy Like a Fox, *among his best two-reel silent shorts of the Twenties (Hal Roach/ Pathé, 1926).*

Another Roach star, Australian-born Harry 'Snub' Pollard, was more-or-less the counterpart of Sennett's Billy Bevan, and was well-known for his Kaiser Wilhelm moustache, worn upside down, and his clever playing of visual gags. His funniest film was probably *It's a Gift* (1923).

In this necessarily short survey of (mostly) American comedy films of the silent period, many names have had to be omitted and many others referred to only in passing. Mr. William Randolph Hearst, for instance, would not care for the fact that no mention is made of his lovely protégée and mistress of many years, Marion Davies, but if he had not led her away from the comedy in which she could be so deliciously effective to more serious stuff, where she was less than good, then she might have had a paragraph or two.

Since comedy and laughter played a big part in movies from the earliest days, it was inevitable that some of it should be lost almost as soon as it was shown in the vaudeville theatres and picture houses of the times. On the other hand, much has since been resurrected by toilers in the deep mines of movie archaeology, so that many players have had, and are still having, their places in the history of movie comedy reassessed.

Take the still little-known Raymond Griffith, one of Paramount's leading comedy players of the 1920s. He had his training in the Mack Sennett comedy funhouse, including writing and directing as well as acting. By the early Twenties, he had settled on acting as his *métier* in the movies, and quickly established an uniquely nonchalant and sophisticated comedy style based on clever situations, sight gags and perfect timing, which never descended into slapstick.

And a supporting player, Griffith stole scenes from Adolphe Menjou in *Open All Night* (1924) and reached real stardom with *Paths to Paradise* in 1925. This film was a big hit in its time, as were Griffith's two films of 1926, *Hands Up*! and *You'd Be Surprised*.

Like many other stars of the Twenties, Griffith failed to surmount the great sound barrier. He had injured his vocal chords some time in the past, and could speak only in a rough whisper. He had a small but effective part as a dying French soldier in *All Quiet on the Western Front* (1930), but after this, although he was involved in film production for some years, there was no more acting. A sad end to the career of an actor whom some critics would place among the very best of comedy stars.

The 'Our Gang' series was begun by Hal Roach in 1922 and continued, with cast changes as the Gang grew up, until 1944. Here, the Gang, including Pete the dog, hold up a bad Injun chief, in reality their director Robert McGowan.

THE ETERNAL THREE:
CHAPLIN, KEATON AND LLOYD

In any survey of movie comedy, the names of three men recur constantly. Each, in his unique way, has become a yardstick by which to measure the performances of other workers in the field. Charles Chaplin's career was both the longest, since it covered over half a century, and the shortest, since he appeared in far fewer films than the other two. Buster Keaton's career, though he appeared in movies right up to the 1960s, was essentially that of the silent movie comic. And Harold Lloyd's was the least 'artistically' perfect of the three, though his films have left us some of the most heart-stopping images of the comic performer in death-defying action.

Charlie Chaplin

English-born Charles Spencer Chaplin (1889-1977) was already famous when he entered the film-making business. The product of a desperately poor childhood, marked by a drunken father and a sick mother whose efforts to keep her children off the rack of poverty and degradation led to her mental breakdown, Chaplin learned to fend for himself at an age when most children are still little more than infants. By the time he was nine, he was earning a living in a travelling dancing act, the Eight Lancashire Lads. Then came work in vaudeville in London, in which direction he had no doubt been pointed by his mother who, like his father, had once been a singer on the vaudeville stage.

In his mid-teens, Charles and his half-brother Sydney Chaplin became members of the Fred Karno pantomime company, one of the best and most popular in England. Charles gradually worked his way up in the company, undertaking tours with it to Europe and America, and by the time of his second trip to the United States in 1913, he was a pretty well-known vaudeville figure, memorable for his 'drunk' act called 'A Night in an English Music Hall': how ironic that a man who all his life would drink little, perhaps as a reaction against his father's drunkenness, should achieve fame as a drunk. Not that the irony bothered him, for Chaplin was to use the act several times in his films, right up to the late feature film *Limelight*.

When Chaplin was appearing with the Fred Karno troupe in New York in 1913, he was spotted by someone from Keystone. Mack Sennett always said that he had been the star-spotter himself, but Mabel Normand also claimed Chaplin as her find. Be that as it may, one day the twenty-four-year-old Chaplin, by now in Philadelphia, received a telegram from Sennett's business partner, Adam Kessel, asking him to come to New York for an interview.

Chaplin was not sure that Keystone's crude brand of slapstick was right for him. On the other hand, the chance to work in films, to widen his experience and his audiences, seemed too good to miss, and the $150.00 a week on offer was twice what he was getting from Fred Karno. By the end of 1913, Chaplin was way out west with the Keystone Film Company and, professionally speaking, he was never to look back.

The Keystone period was short-lived, since he did not extend the one-year contract he had signed at the outset, but it was obviously an important time for Chaplin, for not only was he learning about how films were made, but he was experimenting with acting for a camera, a very different thing from acting for a live audience from behind footlights.

Chaplin's first film, made in three days in 1914, was called *Making a Living*. Even in this relatively mediocre short, it is possible to see hints of how Chaplin would develop his film style for already he was displaying various subtle touches in his acting and in his bits of 'business', such as the use of his cane to hold off someone aiming a punch at him. He also made use of many facial expressions, as well as his wonderfully agile body, to create effects. It was obvious that Chaplin's was to be a more intimate style of acting than that generally followed by the Keystone company.

Chaplin's second film, *Kid Auto Races at Venice*, introduced another aspect of Chaplin's comic style that would be an essential element of his later work. This was his ability to take an inanimate object – in this case, the camera that two men were using to film the races – and turn it into an almost-human foil for his antics. Later objects similarly transformed would include a swinging bar door (*His Favourite Pastime*), a boxing dummy (*Mabel's Married Life*), a whole bakery full of flour, dough and bread (*Dough and Dynamite*), and a foldaway bed (*One A.M.*).

While at Keystone, Chaplin began to develop the Tramp image that would be the most enduring of his screen *personae*. The story goes that Chaplin, in ordinary clothes, was watching Sennett filming with Mabel Normand when the great director, deciding in mid-film that what was needed was more comic business,

Mabel Normand and Charlie Chaplin pursuing a friendship under the stern eyes of Phyllis Allen and Mack Swain in the two-reeler Getting Acquainted *(Keystone/ Mack Sennett, 1914).*

Chaplin making brilliant use of an inanimate object – a folding bed – to provide laughs in One A.M. *(Mutual, 1916).*

shouted to Chaplin to get himself into a funny get-up of some sort and join in the filming. So the skinny little limey, who so far had failed to make any impression at Keystone, dashed off to the dressing-room, picking up here a pair of Fatty Arbuckle's outsize trousers, there a pair of over-large shoes belonging to Ford Sterling, and somewhere else a cane, a derby and a coat that, in hilarious contrast to the baggy pants, was far too small and tight. The moustache was pencilled on, or else was one of Mack Swain's that had been trimmed down – the Tramp's image, if not his character, was conceived.

Although no one else at Keystone was taking much notice of Chaplin in the numerous shorts in which he played, Sennett got word from Kessel in New York, the place where the big film decisions were made since the film world's financial clout was still in the east, that he was pulling in the audiences and Sennett was to keep the Chaplin films coming. Some time after this, Sennett agreed to let Chaplin have a go at writing and directing his own films, and of the thirty-four shorts made at Keystone in 1914, twenty-two, starting with *Caught in the Rain*, were either directed by him alone or co-directed with Mabel Normand.

His thirty-fifth and last film with Keystone was *Tillie's Punctured Romance*. Unlike all those slam-bang shorts, this feature-length film – the first full-length comedy film – took fourteen weeks to make. Marie Dressler took top billing, and Chaplin appeared as a very un-Tramp-like smoothie, looking very dapper for many of his scenes, despite being physically over-whelmed by the vast bulk of the uninhibited Dressler.

Much of what Chaplin did at Keystone was fairly crude, sometimes even showing a streak of cruelty in gags about people being kicked, punched or otherwise ill-treated. But by the time he left the studio to move to Essanay early in 1915, Chaplin had proved his abilities as a film comedian, which Essanay acknowledged in offering him a starting salary of $1,250 a week.

Chaplin was with Essanay for fourteen months and made fourteen shorts, all of which he wrote and directed. In the later ones, starting with *The Tramp*, he explored the intricacies of the Tramp's character, and began to display all the warmth, social concern and sentimentality that were to mark his later films. The guiding philosophy of Chaplin's Tramp was not that 'everything is for the best in the best of all possible worlds,' but that 'where there's life there's hope'. This optimistic belief in a better tomorrow that ended most of the Tramp's adventures, even if he so often and sadly did not come out on top, was what endeared him to audiences and sent them home smiling and happy.

After the Essanay interlude, during which the former San Francisco secretary Edna Purviance became his leading lady, first in a short called *A Night Out*, Chaplin moved to the relatively long-established Mutual company. His contract with them, under which he agreed to make twelve films, gave him $10,000 a week – still a large enough sum in these inflationary days, and almost unheard of in 1916 – plus an outright fee of $150,000 just for putting his signature on the contract. Clearly, Chaplin was being seen as a major force in American movie-making.

Chaplin's films in the nearly two years he was with Mutual have been called his 'Golden Dozen', since all twelve demand to be considered for any list of the finest comedy shorts ever made. Their titles, mostly labels, indicate that Chaplin got his stories from everyday life, usually among the poor and under-privileged – for instance, *The Floorwalker*, *The Fireman*, *The Vagabond*, *The Pawnshop*, *The Rink*, *The Immigrant*.

The Immigrant, among the greatest of the Mutual films, handled a potentially tragic theme – the plight of the thousands of homeless, penniless, friendless immigrants who were washed up on the shores of a seemingly unwelcoming United States every year – with an optimistic humour. Acting with Chaplin in the film were Edna Purviance and the huge, Scottish-born actor, Eric Campbell, who provided the perfect villainous foil to Chaplin's little vagabond in all but one of the Mutual shorts (he died in a car accident in 1917). There was much social criticism, both implied and clearly expressed, in *The Immigrant*, though Chaplin's wonderful visual jokes and comic set-pieces made the film very much a comedy.

The society of the mean streets in a great city's slums turned up again in *Easy Street*, perhaps the best of all Chaplin's Mutual films. The title is an ironic commentary on its subject and the film once again juxtaposed comedy and grim reality to great affect.

By the end of his time with Mutual in 1917, Chaplin was a very wealthy man, with enough financial resources to produce and own the rights in all his pictures from now on. After Mutual, his films were released by First National until he formed his own company, the famous United Artists, with Mary Pickford, Douglas Fairbanks and D. W. Griffith.

Eight more shorts were to be produced between 1918 and 1923. Among them were the brilliant *Shoulder Arms* (1918), with doughboy Charlie coping – or not – with military life and the horrors of war; *Sunnyside* (1918), in which the myth of an idealized country life was parodied; and *The Pilgrim* (1923) in which Charlie appeared in the unlikely role of a preacher in what was to be his last short.

The Kid, released in 1921, was Chaplin's first starring feature film. It was a sentimental tale in which the Tramp found himself becoming a substitute father to a child (Jackie Coogan) abandoned by his mother (Edna Purviance) because she had been taught by society to believe that she, an 'unwed mother', is not fit to bring up her son herself.

Chaplin made three other silent feature films during the 1920s, before sound came along to change everyone's approach to making movies. *A Woman of Paris* (1923) – which Chaplin wrote, directed and produced but did not star in – was essentially a drama, with humorous moments, about a young woman (Purviance) who, separated by circumstances from her true love, goes to Paris, falls from grace and becomes the kept woman of rich Parisian, Adolphe Menjou. Her punishment is to know that her true love commits suicide because of her, and she returns to the countryside to end her days.

Many people found *A Woman of Paris* melodramatic rather than dramatic, and were relieved when Chaplin returned to the screen as the Tramp in *The Gold Rush* (1925). Edna Purviance, having now virtually retired from films (she was to remain on the United Artists payroll until her death in 1958, having had minor roles in *Monsieur Verdoux* and *Limelight*), the delightful Georgia Hale became Chaplin's leading lady in this.

Above: Chaplin and Edna Purviance (left) in his fine short, The Immigrant, *which explored the problems of poor newcomers to America (Mutual, 1917).*

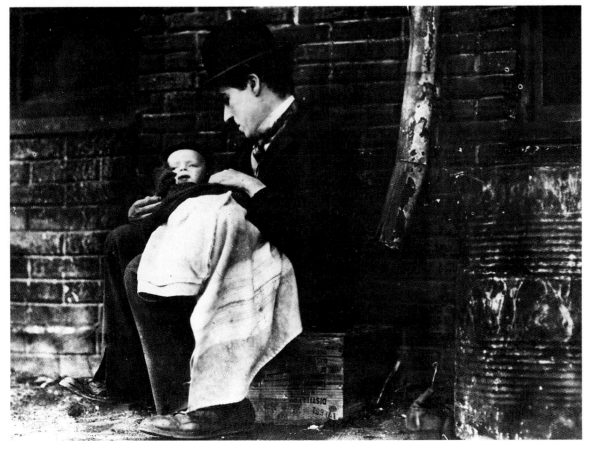

Left: Chaplin in The Kid, *his first starring feature-length film (First National/ Charles Chaplin Corporation, 1921).*

For most people, *The Gold Rush* is one of Chaplin's very best films, interweaving to brilliant effect the pathetic tale of the Tramp's apparently hopeless love for a dance-hall girl with the often wildly funny story of how the Tramp and his gold-prospecting partner (Mark Swain) joined the great Yukon gold rush. Some of the comedy was side-splitting slapstick, some was wonderfully subtle – for instance, the Tramp performing a delightful dance with two bread rolls on forks, or eating with a gourmet's delicacy and pleasure an old boot, boiled up by the starving prospectors. Over it all hangs Chaplin's finely perceived view of the contrast between the Tramp's selfless, humanitarian behaviour and the unpleasant, brutish life of the gold town society.

The Circus, (1928) for which Chaplin won a special Oscar at the first Academy Awards ceremony in 1929, saw the Tramp involved in the life of a travelling circus, attempting numerous acts in it from lion-taming to tight-rope walking, and losing the object of his heart's desire to a much more dashing and handsome man. Once again, the Tramp had to head off alone down the road of life.

Chaplin was in the middle of filming *City Lights* when sychronized sound hit Hollywood. He debated whether to allow the Tramp to talk, but felt that silence best suited his character, and released the film as a 'non-talkie', although with synchronized music and sound effects, in 1931. Since talkies were all the rage by this time, Chaplin was taking a risk, but one that worked, since *City Lights* triumphantly proved that Chaplin's comedy at its best needed no words.

The film, by turns very funny and deeply poignant, counter-pointed the delicate theme of the Tramp's love for a blind girl, played by Virginia Cherrill, with a harsh look at capitalist society's gulf between rich and poor, the overweening power of money and how the need to earn it can degrade a person's humanity. *City Lights'* ending is unforgettably moving: the girl, her sight restored because of the Tramp's selfless generosity, sees him for the first time. The Tramp's reaction, a combination of joy for her and anguish for himself in that the girl may reject him once she can see him, is Chaplin's acting at its greatest.

Chaplin by now was working so slowly that it was 1936 before his next film, *Modern Times*, was released. Once again,

the Tramp did not speak, though he had a gibberish song to sing, and there were sound sequences, including music and a couple of synchronized speaking scenes, added to the film.

It was noticeable that *Modern Times*, despite its memorable comic scenes, notably one in which the assembly-line worker Tramp goes berserk among the machinery, tended to take more seriously the inhumanity of the capitalist system than the laughter-making business in it. This was a trend confirmed in the all-talking *The Great Dictator* (1940), where

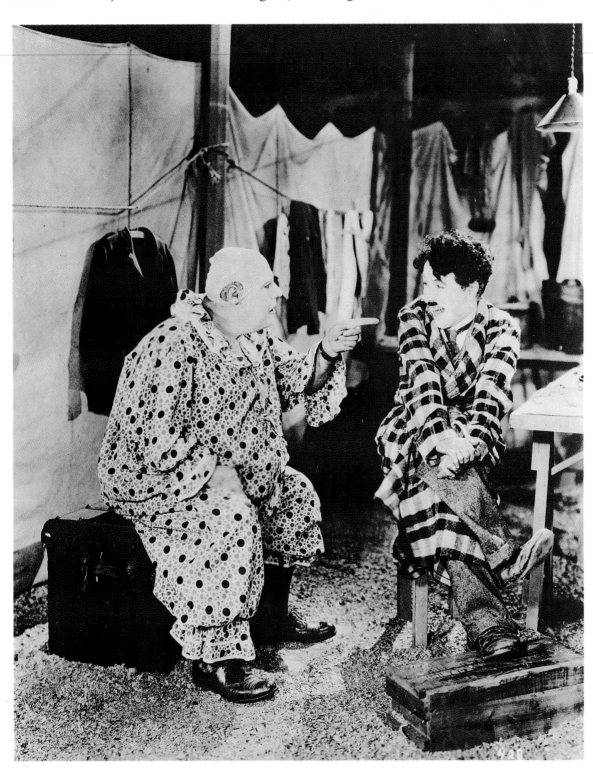

Charles Chaplin, here with Henry Bergman, shows the 'versatility and genius in writing, acting, directing and producing The Circus' *which won him a special Academy Award in 1928 (United Artists/ Charles Chaplin Corporation, 1928).*

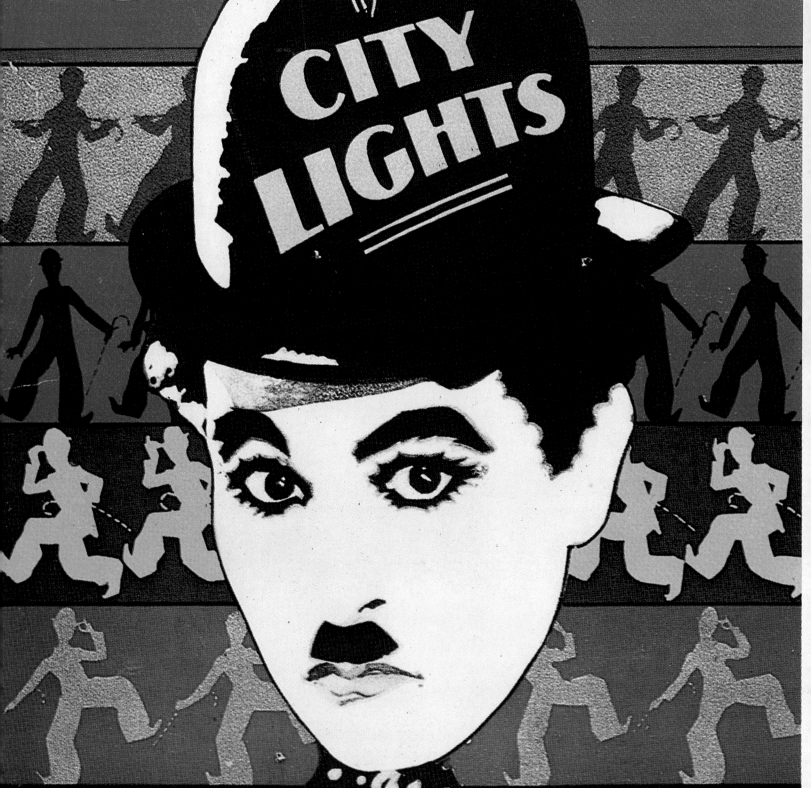

the satire and philosophy – especially in Chaplin's 'curtain speech' – while it did not exactly detract from the ludicrous and very funny lampooning of Hitler (Adenoid Hynkel, one of the two roles played by Chaplin), Mussolini (Benzini Napaloni – the splendid Jack Oakie) and their gangs, certainly felt heavy-handed and even at times out of place. Chaplin either did not recognize that simply comedy on its own could be a very deadly weapon or felt that he wanted to be more than just a clown on film.

He was also by now showing all too clearly his lack of concern for the production values of his films. In sharp contrast to the sophisticated design of sets, scenery and costume displayed by most of the leading film-makers in 1930s and 1940s Hollywood, Chaplin's sets looked as if they had come from a touring theatrical company and had been given a lick of paint before being stuck up in front of his camera.

There had been strong elements of the Tramp in Chaplin's portrayal of the Jewish barber in *The Great Dictator*, but with *Monsieur Verdoux* (1974), in which the comedy was black indeed in its sardonic portrayal of a mass murderer who ends up on the gallows, Chaplin abandoned the Tramp completely. This film, disliked and

Above: The blind flower seller gets to know the man who is going to help her: Chaplin and Virginia Cherrill in City Lights, *written, directed and produced by Chaplin (United Artsts, 1931).*

Left: The Tramp versus the machinery of capitalism: Chaplin's Modern Times *(United Artists/ Charles Chaplin Corporation, 1936).*

Opposite: This poster for Chaplin's City Lights *emphasizes the famous image of The Tramp (United Artists/ Charles Chaplin Corporation, 1931).*

even reviled on its release, has since been reassessed by critics, who have found in it a clever and subtle satirical commentary on a world in which the pressures of society force ordinary, respectable people into behaving against their nature.

Perhaps part of the criticism of *Monsier Verdoux* arose from a desire to attack Chaplin himself, for he had become increasingly the subject of personal abuse in post-war, moralistic America. His private life, with its divorces, paternity suits and scandals, seemed objectionable, his refusal to take United States citizenship was an affront to the nation, and the undoubtedly left-leaning philosophy in his films led people to suspect him of Communist tendencies. The FBI had a file on him, Internal Revenue was pursuing him.

Chaplin left America in 1952, vowing never to return. This was the year in which he made *Limelight*, a bitter-sweet return to his beginnings. The film traced the end of the career and the life of the music-hall comic, Calvero, who had known greatness and fame in the 1880s and 1890s but now (1914) was on the skids. Before he dies – in the wings, offstage – he manages to save the life of a young dancer (Claire Bloom) and set her career on the path to success. The film opens with a replay of Chaplin's great early act based on the action of a drunk man, and indeed, much of the comedy of *Limelight* tends to be in set-pieces, rather than an inherent part of the action, but at its best, it is Chaplin at *his* best. There is a wonderfully comic recital, hilariously performed by Chaplin as the violinist and Buster Keaton as the pianist – the only time the two appeared on film together – and a finely mimed dance of a troupe of performing fleas.

Chaplin's last two films were *A King in New York* (1957), in which he had the main role, and *A Countess from Hong*

When dictators meet ... Chaplin (Hynkel) and Jack Oakie (Napaloni) adopt aggressive poses while Henry Daniell (Garbitsch) looks on in The Great Dictator. *Chaplin's first all-talkie (United Artists/ Charles Chaplin Corporation, 1940).*

Left: Two great men of silent comedy playing brilliantly together for the only time: Buster Keaton and Chaplin make up for their variety act in Limelight *(United Artists/Celebrated Films, 1952).*

Below: A gentleman contemplating his wife – and murder. Chaplin and Martha Raye in Monsieur Verdoux *(United Artists/Charles Chaplin Corporation, 1947).*

Kong (1967) where, apart from a cameo appearance, the seventy-eight-year-old Chaplin left the acting to Marlon Brando and Sophia Loren, contenting himself with writing and directing the film. Neither of Chaplin's last works was very good; both lacked the comic inspiration of the great Chaplin and they look old-fashioned.

Even so, Chaplin's real comic greatness was to be doubly acknowledged in the 1970s. In 1972, welcomed back with huge enthusiasm to an America he had left for good twenty years before, Chaplin was awarded a second special Academy Award for 'the incalculable effect he has had on making motion pictures the art form of this century'. Then, in 1975 Chaplin received a knighthood at the hands of Queen Elizabeth II. It was as an aristocrat of the movies that Sir Charles Chaplin died at his home in Switzerland in 1977.

Buster Keaton

Joseph Francis Keaton (1895-1966), born to travelling show people in Piqua, Kansas, appeared on the boards at an even earlier age than Charlie Chaplin, having joined his parents' acrobatic comedy act at the age of three. He was already known as 'Buster', having been given the nickname by Harry Houdini when he survived unhurt a tumble down the stairs of a show-business boarding-house.

After a childhood and youth spent being thrown about in his family's acrobatic act, Keaton branched out into theatre on his own, partly because the father's drunkenness made the act very unsafe. He was to drift into movies by accident, though his theatrical career made the movies of First World War America, which were gathering in acting and vaudeville talent at an extravagant rate, a not unlikely home for him.

Walking up Broadway one day in 1917, Keaton bumped into a theatre acquaintance who invited him to watch Fatty Arbuckle making a movie. Arbuckle had recently left Keystone and was making his first film on his own, which Joseph Schenck was producing for release by Paramount. Keaton and Arbuckle liked each other on sight and, more or less overnight, Keaton decided to desert the stage, where he had just been offered a star part in a Shubert revue, for films. He joined the team making Arbuckle's first solo short, *The Butcher Boy*, at a studio in a former Manhattan warehouse, and his film career was launched.

He became the complete all-rounder of the film world, equally good as writer, director and comic actor, brilliant at creating gags and superbly athletic in their execution. He also recognized that his greatness lay in his comedy: not for him the role of world philosopher and moral Mr. Fixit that Chaplin attempted. Although near-fanatical in the pursuit of perfection in everything that he did, Keaton did not try to give his comedy any overly serious moral dimension. Where Chaplin took on the ills of society, tilting at the many windmills of strict morality, capitalism and dictatorship – whether of Hitler or the local street cop, café waiter or factory boss – Keaton's comic wrestled with the forces of nature – cyclones, fires, raging rivers – or the larger-than-human mechanical powers of the world, including trains, ships and even whole armies on the march.

Although, unlike Chaplin, Keaton chose to be a comic without a singular personality, there was still plenty of character in his playing. He was an actor whose still, emotionless face topped a body that could accomplish falls, leaps and flips greater, longer and more dangerous than anyone had any right to expect from frail human flesh, but always with apparent ease and considerable grace. Despite this physical brillance, there was, in Keaton's playing, still the sense that the characters he was portraying were an essential part of his whole being, that they really believed and felt what they were doing; it was not just the surface brilliance of an experienced actor.

It was, perhaps, easier for audiences to relate to Keaton's films than to Chaplin's, because Keaton kept his films in the real world. With Chaplin, the viewer is always aware, even if subconsciously, that his characters are usually set against backgrounds made by studio carpenters; there is an air of artificiality and theatricality about his streets and buildings. Not so in Keaton's best films; the settings seem real, the trees rooted in solid earth, the plains really stretching to the horizon, the river running between real banks.

Keaton worked with Fatty Arbuckle's company until 1920, with a few months

*The famous, pale,
emotionless face of a
great comedian:
Buster Keaton in* Go
West *(MGM, 1925).*

off for military service in France towards the end of World War I. He appeared in probably fifteen or sixteen shorts, but since there has never been a definitive list made and many films were lost or not properly recorded at the time, he may have made more.

He took to making films like a duck to water. Although greatly overshadowed by Arbuckle in *The Butcher Boy*, a sort of slapstick ballet in a store, Keaton took every opportunity to put in startling acrobatic gags of his own, such as falling over backwards and spinning on his head before landing on the floor. The titles of most of Keaton's shorts for Arbuckle suggest their basically simple subject matter – *His Wedding Night*, *Fatty at Coney Island*, *Out West*, *The Bell Boy*, *The Cook*, *Back Stage* and numerous others – but by the time Keaton came to make his last film with Arbuckle, *The Garage*, he had become far more than just Arbuckle's sidekick and stooge. He had learned much about film-making, from both sides of the camera, and was ready to branch out on his own.

When Fatty Arbuckle moved on to feature films in 1920, Joseph Schenck set up a company especially to produce a series of Keaton comedy shorts, to be released by Metro and, later, by First National. Under the deal with Schenck, there were nineteen of the so-called 'Keaton Shorts', and one full-length, seven-reel feature film, *The Saphead*, and Keaton wrote, directed and starred in them all. The films were made in Hollywood, where Keaton had moved with Arbuckle towards the end of their joint film-making, at the former Chaplin studios, now renamed the Buster Keaton Studio.

The Saphead was successful enough to make Keaton a real star, but it was less enjoyable than the shorts, perhaps because at this stage in his career, Keaton could not yet control the working through of a full-length story-line. The shorts, on the other hand, were magnificent. In them, Keaton devised a whole new set of guidelines for silent comedy film-makers, with gag following brilliantly honed gag in extravagant quantity and unmatchable quality.

Take *One Week*, for instance, which was only Keaton's second short as his own boss. This concerned the week-long efforts of a handsome young newlywed to put together, from a do-it-yourself kit, a home for his bride. Keaton used one of his best-known gags in this film. The young home-maker is standing in front of his house when suddenly the whole front falls down on top of him. He is saved from being crushed to death by the fact that an open window is in exactly the right place to fall neatly over his shoulders, leaving him standing unscathed and unmoved in the midst of the wreckage. This gag had had an airing before, in an Arbuckle short called *Backstage*, in which Keaton had also played: at one point, the stage scenery fell on to the banjo-playing Arbuckle; once again, the window was in exactly the right place, as it would be again in *Steamboat Bill Jr.*

Then there was that other early Keaton short, *The High Sign* (1920). From its opening shots, this was a non-stop succession of gags, all self-contained but all having their place in the carefully sustained plot. There was the newspaper that, as Keaton turned the pages, unfolded into a bigger and bigger and bigger and, eventually, overwhelming sheet of paper. There was the policeman's gun, stolen by Keaton from its holster on the policeman's hip and replaced by a banana. To bolster Buster's spurious claim to be a great shot (he had got a job in Tiny Tim's Shooting Gallery run, of course, by a giant of a man), Keaton developed a gag about a dog, tied to a wall, grabbing for a bone, pulling a string that releases a lever, that fires a gun, that hits the bull's-eye, that rings a bell . . . .

The climax of *The High Sign* was a chase, this time through a house. The scene was filmed from a distance so that all the rooms of the house, whose outside wall had been cut away, were in frame together. There were revolving doors and walls, hidden trapdoors for people to fall down, drainpipes to be shinned down, stairs to be fallen up – it was a farce at a level that was exhausting for both actors and audience.

In 1923, Keaton moved from shorts to feature-length films. He retained the close-knit unit of cameramen, gag men (of whom he usually employed about four at any one time), designers, technicians and the rest that he had melded together at the Buster Keaton Studio into a team that knew almost instinctively how Keaton's plots should be turned into films.

JOSEPH M. SCHENCK presents

BUSTER KEATON

"THE GENERAL"

LOVE LOCOMOTIVES & LAUGHS

UNITED ARTISTS PICTURE

Together, they made Keaton's very greatest films: *The Three Ages* and *Our Hospitality*, both 1923, *Sherlock, Jr.* and *The Navigator*, both 1924, and *The General* (1926).

The Three Ages was a trio of two-reelers rather than a true feature film, since it consisted of three quite separate, but similar tales of love, set in the Stone Age, ancient Rome and modern times, done in conscious parody of D. W. Griffith's *Intolerance*.

The next feature, *Our Hospitality*, was also a parody, this time of melodramas about feuds between families or rival gangs, and it was a much more cleverly constructed film, with a true dramatic logic, established from its opening scenes, which put the feud in context and accounted for Keaton's involvement in it, to its climax. This film also looked good, partly because Keaton had chosen to film

it in the great outdoors of the Nevada country. One of the actresses in it was Keaton's young wife, Natalie Talmadge, sister of Norma, whom he had married in 1921.

The extraordinarily imaginative *Sherlock, Jr.* was a virtuoso performance by Keaton the comic actor and Keaton the director. In this film, he played a cinema projectionist who becomes so involved in the films he is screening that he imagines he is actually taking part in the action. He finds that he has great trouble in keeping separate the imaginary world of the screen and the real world of his own everyday life.

This almost surrealistic film was followed by *The Navigator*, which was to bring Keaton greater commercial success than he had known hitherto. Its story was built round a deserted schooner, on which Keaton developed a glorious sequence of nautical scenes and actions.

One of Buster Keaton's greatest films, The General, *was a tale of the Civil War, with a train playing a leading role (United Artists/Schenk, 1926).*

Keaton and Ernest Torrence contemplating Mississippi riverboat life in Steamboat Bill, Jr. *(United Artists/ Buster Keaton Productions, 1928).*

The General, said to be Keaton's own favourite among his films, and the one in which a train had a starring role, evoked beautifully the Civil War period in which it was set. It is also outstanding for the integrity with which it was made. There was nothing slapdash or comic about the finely wrought tale, or the way in which the drama was played out. The comedy became an integral part of the story, not just a series of funny turns tacked on to it.

Keaton, working solo with his own company, made only two more films – *College* (1927) and *Steamboat Bill, Jr.* (1928) – before his career took a disastrous turn from which it never recovered. Joseph Schenck sold Keaton's contract to Metro-Goldwyn-Mayer. Rather than maintain his independence, Keaton signed

with Metro-Goldwyn-Mayer. His own production team was disbanded and he himself was swallowed up in the Hollywood studio system at its most powerful.

At first, things did not go too badly, and *The Cameraman* (1928) and *Spite Marriage* (1929) had much in them of Keaton's great talent. But he disliked the lack of freedom of the studio system, the lack of control over his own work, the insensitivity of the bosses to his style of filmmaking. He began to go downhill: his drinking, always heavy, teetered over into alcoholism, and his marriage faltered, ending in divorce in 1932. His later films degenerated into stuff almost too bad to contemplate, especially the ones that showed glimpses of what Keaton could do when at his best. Sound did not help

either, especially MGM-type sound with its emphasis on super-glossy production values that swamped Keaton's carefully planned, subtly executed work.

Louis B. Mayer sacked Keaton in 1933. During the rest of the Thirties and early Forties, he kept body and soul more or less together – there were bouts of mental breakdown and a period in a psychiatric clinic – with two-reel shorts for Educational Pictures and Columbia. Unlike Chaplin or Harold Lloyd, Keaton had not kept control over or ownership of his films, so he never had enough money to set up on his own again.

In the late Forties, a revival of the Keaton legend began that had still not peaked by the time of his death from cancer in 1966. He made a series of live appearances at the Cirque Medrano in Paris and appeared to telling effect in Billy Wilder's *Sunset Boulevard* (1950) and Chaplin's *Limelight* (1952), and the world was suddenly sitting up and taking notice of the great man from the golden days of silent film comedy. Invitations to appear on television chat shows and in series, in films, at retrospectives of his films began pouring in from all over the world. A film biography, *The Buster Keaton Story* (1957), starring Donald O'Connor, was drear but provided a fee for Keaton large enough to give him financial security, and there were many more parts, big and small, in American and European films right until his death. Life's great roller-coaster seemed to have come to the top for Keaton in the end.

One of Keaton's last really great comedy features was The Cameraman, *in which he learned about being a news film photographer (MGM/ Buster Keaton Productions, 1928).*

Harold Lloyd

There was no theatrical blood flowing through the veins of Harold Lloyd (1893-1971) – unlike Chaplin and Keaton, he was not 'born in a trunk'. His father seems to have been an unsuccessful sort, or perhaps just unlucky in business. He had tried out photography and pool-hall ownership before moving from Nebraska, where Harold had been born, to try his luck in San Diego, California.

There must have been some instinct for acting in young Harold's genes, however, for he was soon lurking round the local theatres, doing odd jobs and gradually getting drawn into the world of the stage. While still in his teens, he began getting acting jobs with touring companies and stock theatres. Before long, he had gravitated towards the movies and to Hollywood where the orange and avocado groves were already in danger from the burgeoning film industry. Colonel Bill Selig had opened the first big film studio in Hollywood 1909, and Cecil B. De Mille would descend on the place in 1913, taking over a stable for his first studio.

Harold Lloyd first capered in front of a movie camera in 1912, playing a half-naked Indian brave as an extra at Edison. Then he went to Keystone and worked in one or two of their comedies before moving on to Universal, where he became friendly with another extra and stuntman called Hal Roach.

Young Roach had ambitions to be a film producer and director and, when he inherited a few thousand dollars, saw that his moment had come. He set up his own outfit, and asked Harold Lloyd to join him, offering him the name part in a series of comedy shorts about a character called Willie Work.

We cannot assess today what the shorts were like for they seem to have vanished without trace. They were probably fairly poor for, after all, both Roach and Lloyd were novices in film and Lloyd had neither the stage training nor the years of experience that had enabled both Chaplin and Keaton to make worthwhile and noticeable contributions to their first films. The fact that Roach could not find a distributor interested enough in the shorts to take them on also suggests that they were not very good. Roach and Lloyd separated and went their own ways.

Lloyd returned to Keystone, but failed to make any impression on Mack Sennett, and when Roach found himself a new sponsor in Pathé, Lloyd moved back to him with alacrity.

The next character that the two developed together was rather more successful than Willie Work – in fact, Lonesome Luke became quite famous in 1916/17 – but on the whole, the Lonesome Luke series does not look up to much today. The resemblance to – indeed, the wholesale copying of – Chaplin's Tramp is obvious, with Lloyd as Lonesome Luke dressed up in a tight coat and ill-fitting trousers, little moustache, a cane and odd-shaped shoes. There the resemblance ended, for Lloyd was incapable of the delicate nuances Chaplin could get into his characterizations, and neither Lloyd nor Roach had much idea of using film to tell stories that made comments on the human condition as Chaplin did.

What Lloyd was good at was the basic physical knockabout stuff that was such a staple ingredient of comedy shorts at this time. Lloyd's and Roach's Lonesome Luke films were all about Luke in some sort of physical bother, and there was a great deal of kicking, punching, bumping, throwing heavy objects at each other and running round park benches, with Lloyd making up in energy and enthusiasm for what he lacked in experience and skill. That these shorts were made as quickly and cheaply as possible is indicated by the fact that the Lloyd-Roach team turned out something like 200 one- and two-reelers between 1915 and 1919. In them, Lloyd was supported more often than not by the teenage Bebe Daniels (who began taking adult roles at the age of fourteen) as his leading lady, Snub Pollard as his friend or sidekick and Bud Jamison as the villain or heavy.

It could take about one working week – and in those days a working week could be seven days long – to make a Lonesome Luke film, which in its earliest days was a ten-minute one-reeler. There would be no script, just a few ideas for gags floating about in the air and needing something to anchor them down. The Lonesome Luke film titles give an indication of what the anchors, or story-lines, could be: *Luke Lugs Luggage*, *Luke and the Bomb Throwers*, *Luke's Society Mix-Up*, *Luke: Crystal Gazer*, *Luke Joins the Navy*, *Luke*

and the Mermaids, Luke the Chauffeur,
Luke the Gladiator, Lonesome Luke:
Lawyer, Luke Wins Ye Ladye Fair, Lonesome Luke: Plumber, and so on and so
on.

By late 1919, Harold Lloyd had had
enough of all this and was looking for
something better, and he found it, surprisingly enough, in a pair of horn-rimmed
glasses and a straw boater. In other
words, he exchanged the by-now traditional style of the movie slapstick clown
for something more akin to the average
American young man. At first the 'glasses'
character appeared in shorts very similar
to the Lonesome Luke ones: indeed, for a
time Lloyd alternated the two in his output. After a few insignificant one-reelers,
the new character began to develop a life
and believability of its own. Harold Lloyd
in glasses would eventually become a real
person, whereas Harold Lloyd in moustache and funny clothes was never more
than a clown, a caricature. But he had at
least been serving an apprenticeship in all
those shorts, having made far more than
either Chaplin or Keaton had done at a
similar stage in their film careers, and so
was able to make good use of the opportunity that Roach gave him in the form of
increasingly better stories and more finely
crafted films.

By the early 1920s, when he at last began making feature films, Harold Lloyd was well on the way to becoming one of the funniest and most popular stars in American films. By the mid-Twenties he would achieve world-wide recognition and one of the biggest salaries in Hollywood – a far cry from the time of the failure of the Willie Work series in 1914-15 when Roach had refused to double his salary from $5 to $10 a week. (Chaplin at this time was being paid $1,250 a week by Essanay.)

Lloyd's long run of comedy shorts, of which about 150 had to be made before they stopped looking little better than crude, came to an end in 1921 with the making of his first feature, *A Sailor-Made Man*. By this time, Lloyd and Roach had learned how to meld the disparate collection of largely unrelated gags that had characterized the Lonesome Luke shorts into a compact unity of story and gag. Harold Lloyd's feature films were also notable for the careful way in which the gags and comic set-pieces were plotted in detail before they were filmed. They would even be refilmed if try-outs before an audience showed that they were not getting the expected laughs. Thus, a certain cold-eyed professionalism replaced the jolly spontaneity of the early shorts, and to the modern eye, there is a lack of emotional involvement in much of Harold Lloyd's work, and less to respond to than in the work of Chaplin or Keaton or at his best, Harry Langdon.

The enormous importance of a prop or bit of costume was also a characteristic of Lloyd's own acting. It is quite common for an actor to need to have some external feature of the character he or she is to play – perhaps the shoes, or the shape of the nose, or the way he or she walks – firmly in the actor's mental grasp before the whole character can be created. But with Lloyd, the glasses *were* the character; with a Lloyd film character, we do not feel that there is anything more worth discovering behind the horn-rimmed glasses, as we well know there is in a Chaplin or Keaton *persona*. Nor does Lloyd's character seem to be telling us much about life, or commenting upon it: he seems to exist in a special sort of vacuum called 'Lloydland', unique to him.

While this may affect our historic view of Lloyd's films, it certainly was not

bothering his world-wide audiences in the 1920s. His films made millions laugh – when they were not gasping with fright at his stunts.

Harold Lloyd once defined his films as falling into two categories: either they were 'situation' pictures or they were 'story' pictures. Two of his early features highlight the difference. *Grandma's Boy*, made in 1922, is a story picture. At the beginning, a weak and timorous young

man is unable to do anything about a rough tramp who is terrorizing the neighbourhood. His grandmother, who has already had to see off the tramp herself with the aid of a broom, tells Harold about his grandfather, also a quiet, peace-loving sort of man who became a hero of the Civil War because a gipsy gave him a magic charm, which Grandma still happens to have about her. Harold takes it, and is able to overcome the villainous tramp and his rival for his girlfriend's affections, a tough chap who had thrown Harold down a well at the start of the film and now gets pushed down the same well himself by the magic-invigorated Harold. Eventually Harold finds that his charm is just an old umbrella handle; Grandma had been applying a bit of psychology. All in all, this is an entertaining and agreeable film with a satisfactory outcome to an interestingly told story.

Harold Lloyd, supported by Grandma (Anna Townsend), wonders how he is going to cope with the bullying tramp (Dick Sutherland) in Grandma's Boy (Hal Roach/Associated Exhibitors, 1922).

Harold Lloyd in trouble again, this time at the bottom of the heap in the college football match which was the high point of The Freshman *(Pathé/ Harold Lloyd Corporation, 1925).*

The perfect example of the 'situation' film is *Safety Last*, made a year later and one of Harold Lloyd's most famous pictures. As a film, it is less satisfactory than *Grandma's Boy* because it spends most of its length leading up in a not very entertaining way to the last-reel climax that made it famous: Harold's climb up the outside of a skyscraper, an episode that must be one of the best combinations of hilarious gag and breathless thrill in movies. Lloyd had used the building-ledge gag in the earlier shorts *Ask Father* and *Look Out Below* (both 1919) and *High and Dizzy* (1920), but they were mere rehearsals for what was to come now. Surely no one has ever bettered *Safety Last's* immortal shot of Harold Lloyd holding on to the minute hand of the building's clock as it inevitably, inexorably turns to point to the ground all those floors below. Then the clock's face falls forward to hang over the street... Was there a single heart anywhere in Lloyd's audiences that did not miss several beats?

Among Lloyd's eighteen feature films – of which the last was *The Sins of Harold Diddlebock*, better known by the title under which it was re-issued in 1947, *Mad Wednesday* – the best was probably *The Freshman* (*College Days* in UK), a silent movie issued in 1925. This is the story of a college boy of no importance and a football player of such small ability that he is permitted only to sit on the substitutes' bench as the water boy. He eventually gets on the field and, at the end of the funniest game ever seen on the screen, scores the vital touchdown.

Harold Lloyd's sound features were generally much more successful, both critically and with audiences, than either Keaton's or Chaplin's during the same period. He kept his stories light and entertaining, attempting none of the Chaplin moralizing. *Movie Crazy* (1932) is generally thought to be about the best of his 1930s output even though, since it was filled with wonderfully planned and executed gags, it was still very much in the silent film tradition.

The triumphant climax of *The Freshman* became the opening scene of Lloyd's last film twenty-two years later, *Mad Wednesday*, in which the football hero has now become a bent, prematurely old clerk about to be pensioned off early. The film is about his re-awakening to the joys of life. After this Lloyd now retired gracefully and without fanfare to live in wealthy retirement for the rest of his days, only emerging into the public gaze in the early 1960s to launch two successful compilations of his films, *Harold Lloyd's World of Comedy* (1962) and *Harold Lloyd's Funny Side of Life* (1963), which introduced a new young audience to the brilliance of Harold Lloyd's comedy.

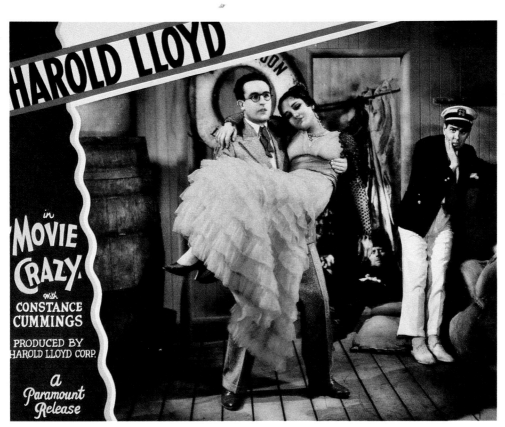

Left: Harold Lloyd *appears to have got the girl (Constance Cummings) in* Movie Crazy *(Paramount/Harold Lloyd Corporation, 1932).*

Below: Harold Lloyd *extending his exploration of the possibilities of film comedy in the air in* Feet First *(Paramount/Harold Lloyd Corporation, 1930).*

NOTHING SACRED:
THE COMEDY FILM IN THE 1930s

The coming of sound to the movies at the end of the 1920s changed the nature of film comedy as profoundly as it changed the cinema as a whole. Sound made movies more sophisticated and more attractive to a wider audience. It has been estimated that some 57 million people went to the movies in America in 1927, the year after synchronized sound was introduced by Warner Brothers, first in John Barrymore's *Don Juan*, and then in Al Jolson's *The Jazz Singer*, but by 1929 cinema attendances across the United States had almost doubled, and sound had come to stay. Cinema owners found sound film so popular that they were able to afford without difficulty the cost of installing the new sound equipment, and by 1930 there were hardly any cinemas on both sides of the Atlantic that were not wired for sound.

If sound turned out to be a bad thing for any group in particular, it was for those film actors, some of them of worldwide fame, whose voices and/or acting ability did not fit. Comedians, who for a long time had had comfortable niches in the comedy shorts of the 1920s, were hardest hit, especially those whose reputation had been based on their abilities as visual performers, whose training had all been in expressing themselves physically but not verbally, and whose films had been tailored to this. Comic actors who could not deliver a funny remark or a quick wisecrack or handle amusing dialogue found their screen careers abruptly ended.

For a time, too, the international exchange value of comedy was considerably reduced. American accents did not go down well in Britain – where the home-grown product was actually advertised on occasion as being 'spoken with all the charm and purity of the English voice' – nor were British accents acceptable in America, while neither was any use in Europe and other non-English-speaking parts of the world. By the same token, the market in America for films from Italy, France, Germany and other foreign film-producing countries more or less dried up for a time, and would never again be as wide open as it had been in the innocent early days of the movies.

However, if the foreigner could speak English charmingly and was willing to work away from home, then his chances of making it with American or British audiences improved considerably. One of these was Maurice Chevalier who, coming from France to star with Jeanette Mac-Donald in Lubitsch's *The Love Parade* in 1929, became one of the first sound movie stars to have a really international career.

It was not just words that comedians were having to come to terms with, but music as well, for the first sound pictures relied heavily on music to fill the vacuum, partly because the movie-makers were still ironing out the troubles they were having with recording human voices. The words had to be spoken carefully into large, strategically placed microphones, a virtual impossibility for quick-moving slapstick comedians.

Thus, in the very early days of sound, comedy if found at all in feature films, was likely to be something sandwiched in between the big production numbers in the 'musical comedies' and revues, many of them lifted off the Broadway stage, that flooded into cinemas around 1930: the first feature-length musical, released in 1929, was actually called *Broadway Melody*. Two other Broadway shows

MAURICE CHEVALIER in "The Love Parade"

A Paramount ERNST LUBITSCH Production WITH JEANETTE MacDONALD

filmed in 1929 were *Hit the Deck*–'a musical extravaganza in which flashes of sheer humour mingle with stirring drama' – and *Rio Rita*, starring Bebe Daniels and John Boles, which brought two Broadway comedians, Bert Wheeler and Robert Woolsey, into films for the first but not for the last time, since they were to appear in a long list of films in the 1930s as a wise-cracking duo in the Abbott and Costello mould. *The Love Parade* was a spectacular-looking musical comedy directed with wit and style by Ernst Lubitsch, and in 1933, *Footlight Parade* was distinguished by a quick-fire performance from James Cagney whose style of comedy was more verbal than physical.

Eddie Cantor was another Broadway personality whose film career, which had begun none too auspiciously in silent films, blossomed in the early years of the sound musical comedy, so that by 1933,

when he was a big star both in films and on the radio in the United States, he was the highest paid comedian in the country. His first important feature was *Palmy Days* (1931), which had quite a strong comedy plot amid the songs and big production numbers. The million-dollar-budgeted *The Kid from Spain* (1932) got its comedy from the sight of a big-eyed little Eddie having to pose as a bullfighter in Mexico while at the same time fending off the attentions of an aggressive female. Busby Berkeley choreographed the impressive production numbers, which involved dozens of the famed Goldwyn Girls.

Roman Scandals, which appeared in 1933, was the best of the Cantor film vehicles made for Sam Goldwyn. The story-line this time had Cantor, a young man from West Rome, Oklahoma, with a great interest in ancient Rome, day-

By the time Maurice Chevalier starred in his second American movie, Lubitsch's The Love Parade, *he had become Hollywood's favourite Frenchman. Jeanette MacDonald seems more bemused than enchanted (Paramount, 1929).*

dreaming his way back to Roman times and imagining how he would have handled things if he had been in a position of power in those far-off days. Once again Busby Berkeley had a hand in making this an incredibly glamorous-looking movie. As always, there were girls by the dozen – some of them wearing nothing but long blonde tresses (they were supposed to be Roman slaves) and many more just lightly clad in glittering bras and diaphanous skirts – and there were five great songs by Al Dubin and Harry Warren. In the midst of all this, Eddie Cantor, often in black face, played the rather low, distinctly lascivious comedy with gusto.

Around 1930, the great silent comedians were all involving themselves with sound, with Chaplin's *City Lights* (1931) making the smallest concessions to the new era. Harold Lloyd, whose first talkie, reshot after starting out as a silent movie, proved quite adept at blending the old and new styles, and his second talkie, *Feet First* (1930), was a clever blending of thrill and gag, with not too much of the strictly visual in the gags.

Keaton and Langdon fared the worst. Keaton actually performed song-and-dance routines in his first talkie, *Free and Easy* (1930), a title that did not reflect reality, for Keaton did not handle the admittedly badly written dialogue well, and he looked wooden, as if he no longer felt himself master of the situation. Langdon, who had been bankrupted in 1928, tried a talkie 'comeback' in 1929, making two-reelers for Hal Roach, but he sounded like a simpleton, and after eight shorts his contract was terminated. He tried again for Educational Pictures in 1932, again making cheap two-reelers, and moved from there to Columbia where there were occasional flashes of good work among the mediocre shorts. In fact, Langdon kept on working right up to the time of his death from a stroke in 1944, by which time those who remembered him in his great silent comedy days could feel only sadness at the tragic fall from fame of the little man who never really understood why he was not any good any more.

The two-reel comedy short was another casualty of the new era. With the double bill becoming the fashion, there was no room on cinema programmes for the all-action comic turn, even if the film-makers offered to give them away free as an inducement to take their feature films. They survived into the 1930s, most notably in the work of Laurel and Hardy (discussed in the next chapter) and Charlie Chase for Hal Roach, but on the whole, their day was done with the coming of sound.

Charlie Chase is, in fact, one of the unsung heroes of early comedy, this because much of his work was behind the scenes and went unrecognized. Under his real name of Charles Parrott, he was a good director of silent shorts: as director-general of the Roach studio, he directed numerous Snub Pollard shorts, over-saw the production of the early Our Gang films, and directed Will Rogers' first short for Roach, *Jes' Passin' Through* (1923). He returned to acting in the mid-Twenties and had little trouble making the transition to sound, since he had a good voice, and could even sing a little. What he did not do was make the transition to feature films, and apart from small parts in two features in the 1930s, he stayed in the confined world of the two-reel comic short. He made nearly sixty shorts for Hal Roach, some of which he also directed, between 1929 and 1936, when Roach phased out short-film production. He then moved to Columbia to make another twenty between 1937 and 1940, the year in which the hard-drinking Chase died of a heart attack, aged forty six.

He had written many of the scripts for his Columbia shorts, his speciality, at which he was very inventive, being the situation comedy, a format within which he could develop clever stories and gags. The studio acknowledged their worth by re-using them in films with the likes of Billy Gilbert, Andy Clyde and Bert Wheeler.

Once the initial teething troubles of putting sound into pictures had been ironed out, which they were remarkably quickly, everything was ready to make the 1930s the great age of talkies comedy. Perversely, the Great Depression helped: the movies were an unbeatable form of escapism, tickets were cheap and attendance figures sky-rocketed everywhere. While musical comedy was a particularly lavish form of escapism, the laugh-in-every-line comedy of words and wit was just as good – perhaps better, because audiences could be more involved, by laughing with rather than just looking at what was being shown on the screen.

Two distinct strands may be seen in the comedy films that came out of Hollywood in the 1930s, which set the style and pace for the rest of the films of the Western world. There was the sophisticated, mildly satirical comedy, culminating in the slapstick, screwball comedies of the late 1930s, in which the battle of the sexes and a certain anti-romantic cynicism added a witty spice. And there was the more family-orientated 'folksy' comedy, typified at the beginning of the period by the films of Will Rogers and at the end by the Andy Hardy films of Mickey Rooney, with Shirley Temple (who made nine films in 1934 alone) adding sentiment to the middle of the decade.

Threaded through both kinds of comedy was the rise of team comedy, at its greatest in the films of the Marx Brothers, Laurel and Hardy and, later, Abbot and Costello, but with lesser combinations such as the Ritz Brothers (three singing and dancing brothers who provided much entertainment in lowish budget Fox musicals), Wheeler and Woolsey, Olsen and Johnson (a vaudeville pair of generally modest account in movies, but with one big hit in the lunatic *Hellzapoppin'* of 1941), Clark and McCullough and The Three Stooges, all providing the spirit of laughter in dozens of comedy films.

Marie Dressler and Wallace Beery were not exactly a team, since they made only two films together, plus *Dinner at Eight*, in which they both appeared though not as a twosome, but they were outstanding as a combined force. Both had had long, and in Marie's case at least, distinctly chequered acting careers when MGM teamed them together in *Min and Bill*

There were some near-scandalous costumes as well as popular comedian Eddie Cantor to catch the eye in Roman Scandals *(United Artists/Samuel Goldwyn, 1933).*

(1930), Marie coming to this one from her fine performance as a waterfront hag in Garbo's *Anna Christie*. The tragi-comedy *Min and Bill* won Marie Dressler an Oscar as best actress that year. She and Beery were teamed up again in 1933, in *Tugboat Annie*, as a couple of old waterfront types; Annie (Dressler) has to take over the captaincy of their tugboat when husband Terry (Beery) becomes too alcoholic to cope, in a film that is, by turns, sad, funny, sentimental and down-to-earth.

The greatest exponent of sophisticated, witty comedy of sexual manners was, of course, Mae West, whose buxom, hour-glass shape sashayed through eight tales of sexual *double entendre* and innuendo in the Thirties. Born in 1892, the daughter of a heavyweight boxer, she had begun her long acting career by the time she was five, and was in vaudeville in New York from her early teens. She soon began writing her own material, and was still doing so in 1970 when she wrote her dialogue for *Myra Breckinridge*. The first Broadway play written, produced and directed by her, in 1926, was succinctly called 'Sex' – and was shut down by the law, which sent its author to jail for ten days on an obscenity charge. Mae shrugged that off soon enough and by 1928 was back on Broadway with the first of three big hits, 'Diamond Lil'.

Clearly made for talkies, Mae West was signed up by Paramount. Her first film was *Night After Night* (1932) in which West's not very important part was given immediate impact by the actress's fully formed and powerful screen personality.

Marie Dressler hitting the peak of a long career, and winning an Oscar, in Min and Bill. *Not liking the sound of things is Wallace Beery (MGM, 1930).*

'Goodness,' said the hat-check girl to Mae on her first appearance at George Raft's club, 'what lovely diamonds!' 'Goodness had nothing to do with it, dearie,' replied Miss West, and a star and a legend were born.

Night After Night was followed by the starring role in the film adaptation of 'Diamond Lil' – *She Done Him Wrong* (1933) – in which she looked under her preposterous eyelashes at Cary Grant, flicked her hip, and said, 'Come up and see me sometime.' It was no studio hack's gag; in all her films, Mae wrote her own dialogue and usually contributed to the script as well, coming up with such lines as 'It's not the men in my life that count; it's the life in my men,' or more outrageously, 'Is that a gun in your pocket or are you just pleased to see me?' or 'Beulah, peel me a grape.' Paramount were happy to let Mae West do the writing, despite the fulminations of the Hollywood

censors, for *She Done Him Wrong* took $2 million at the box office, at a time when the studio's finances were very shaky.

The film also aroused such controversy that it led directly to the imposition of the Hollywood Production Code, with its emphasis on 'morals' and its watering down of the strong sexual innuendo that coloured Mae West's style. Not that Mae West was greatly troubled, since she could imply as much in her delivery as she could in her dialogue. Throughout the Thirties, her films continued to attract huge audiences, despite the fact that none of them quite matched *She Done Him Wrong* and its successor, *I'm No Angel*, which also starred Cary Grant, for sharp wit and pace. *Klondike Annie* (1936), for instance, suffered much from the blue pencil of the Production Code office, while the much heralded confrontation with W. C. Fields, the great anti-hero of

Alison Skipworth seems less than happy with the company of Mae West and George Raft in Night After Night *(Paramount, 1932).*

63

American films, in *My Little Chickadee* (1940) was something of a damp squib, with neither star able to give together the sharp-edged performance they achieved solo.

On paper, the combination of West and W. C. Fields, the great misanthrope, child and dog hater and alcohol lover, should have been dynamite. Like West, William Claude Fields, born Dukenfield, had had a long career in vaudeville, at the outset of which he had been so skilled a juggler that he had plans to become the world's greatest. Eventually he became a genuine Broadway star, playing in such famous shows as the 'Ziegfield Follies' and the 'George White Scandals.' He took his vaudeville skills and the acts he had developed into silent films but was not very successful, coming into his own only with the advent of sound.

The talkies allowed people to hear that splendid, rasping, Falstaffian voice, which gave an extra, essential dimension to Fields' characterizations of men generally at odds with the world. Often, he played a con-man, a card-sharp with four aces up his sleeve, or a family man at odds with wife, children, neighbours and the world in general. Whatever it was, Fields was against it.

It's a Gift (1934) was the best example of the Fields character as the hapless family man, beset by nagging wife, dreadful son and petty customers in his small-town grocery store. This was the film that featured one of Fields's most famous scenes in which the harassed husband is forced, after an argument with his wife, to sleep on the porch – or at least try to, for a series of increasingly wild incidents make sleep an impossibility. The twelve-minute scene was a hilariously funny portrait of frustration.

The Bank Dick (*The Bank Detective* in UK, 1940) is generally considered to be Fields' masterpiece, largely because he had left Paramount for the smaller, more informal Universal Studios where he could do as he liked, so long as it was not expensive. In *The Bank Dick* he was Egbert Sousé, a man with a weakness for telling tall tales about his past – 'Can't get the celluloid out of my blood,' he booms while spinning a yarn about his days directing Arbuckle, Chaplin *and* Keaton in their movies – and a fondness for alcohol, much of which is drunk in a

dubious-looking saloon called the Black Pussy Cat away from his awful shabby-genteel family. By the end of the film, Sousé's luck has transformed them all from respectable poverty to vulgar wealth, and the American Protestant work ethic has been turned on its head, for no honest toil has gone into this financial advancement.

After *The Bank Dick* came Fields' last film in which he had a starring role, *Never give a Sucker an Even Break* (*What a Man* in UK, 1941), said to have been worked out by Fields on the back of an envelope while sitting on the lavatory. A distasteful thought? Well, it was a pretty tasteless, as well as rambling, incoherent, discursive, and inept movie about the making of movies. It started off with a good enough visual gag cutting Hollywood pretension down to size – Fields

Above: Franklin Pangborn and W. C. Fields sensing trouble at the bank in The Bank Dick *(Universal, 1940).*

Opposite: Mae West and W. C. Fields hardly sparkled together in My Little Chickadee, *so the film was a 'last' as well as a 'first' for this intriguing team (Universal, 1940).*

is seen standing outside the gate of Universal Studios, on which is displayed a large poster of the great star W. C. Fields in *The Bank Dick*, and being ignored by everyone passing by – and went on to develop a 'plot' about the creating of a plot for a Hollywood movie. The whole dreadful shambles ended with an apparently irrelevant chase of the Keystone Kops variety.

W. C. Fields' great contribution to American movie comedy, apart from his own outsize personality, was a debunking of pretension, in which he used a cynical and unsentimental humour to mock dishonest and false bourgeois respectability – and if *that* sounds pretentious, at least Mr. Fields, having long since been gathered in by 'the old man in the bright nightgown', is no longer around to deliver a comprehensive putdown.

As for Mae West, if she contributed anything to movie-making in the 1930s apart from sex, it was the death blow she dealt the Hollywood myth of the sweet little heroine who must always be innocent and good. The female stars of the best Hollywood comedies of that decade could give as good as they got, could be wise-cracking, cigarette-smoking martini drinkers if they wanted, could even confess to a sin or two and remain very definitely the heroines. Not for them a melodramatic casting into outer darkness, there to earn the wages of sin. The genre also allowed them to make fools of themselves, and in fact, the sophisticated comedy of the 1930s seems in retrospect to be a parade of tall, rangy, beautiful women of strong character and independent spirit: Myrna Loy, who starred with William Powell and a wire-haired terrier

Movie queen Carole Lombard is obviously paying too close attention to director Charles Lane to please the jealous impresario John Barrymore in Twentieth Century *(Columbia, 1934).*

THE CAST

William Powell............................Godfrey
Carole Lombard........................Irene Bullock
Alice Brady..........................Angelica Bullock
Gail Patrick.........................Cornelia Bullock
Jean Dixon.................................Molly
Eugene Pallette...............Alexander Bullock
Alan Mowbray......................Tommy Gray
Mischa Auer................................Carlo
Robert Light.......................Faithful George
Pat Flaherty................................Mike

WITH
ALICE   GAIL   JEAN
BRADY · PATRICK · DIXON
Based on the novel by Eric Hatch · Screenplay by Morrie Ruskind and Eric Hatch · Directed by Gregory La Cava

CHAS. R. ROGERS
EXECUTIVE PRODUCER
A UNIVERSAL PICTURE

called Asta in *The Thin Man*; Jean Arthur, who brought great style to her 'Cinderella' role in *Easy Living* (1937); Katharine Hepburn, who was Cary Grant's sparring partner in three vintage Thirties comedies, *Holiday*, *Bringing Up Baby* and *The Philadelphia Story*; Irene Dunne, Rosalind Russell and the lovely, blonde Carole Lombard. Among them, they appeared in comedies as grown-up and sophisticated as anything ever made in Hollywood.

The glamorous Lombard received her early comedy-film training in the Mack Sennett school, playing with such pros as Billy Bevan, Chester Conklin and Mack Swain in numerous slapstick two-reelers in the late Twenties. Such training was to stand her in good stead when she came up against the splendid John Barrymore in *Twentieth Century* (1934), one of the earliest of the so-called 'screwball' comedies of the Thirties, and a very funny film

indeed. The basic plot concerned a clash of two giant theatrical egos, as the actress/filmstar Lombard battled, sometimes physically, with the impressario/film director Barrymore. Theirs was a love story, but a sophisticated one in which the wit and comedy arising out of people's characters were what mattered, not sentimental, rose-entwined happy endings.

Among Lombard's later films, three comedies were outstanding: *My Man Godfrey* (1936), in which William Powell was Godfrey; William Wellman's *Nothing Sacred* (1937), with Lombard intent on a final fling because she thinks she's dying of radium poisoning, a black comedy attack on the hypocrisy of newspapers and their readers scripted by Ben Hecht; and Ernst Lubitsch's *To Be or Not to Be* (1942), finished just before Lombard, then married to Clark Gable, was killed in a plane crash.

Carole Lombard rescued gentleman-bum William Powell from a rubbish heap and made him her butler in My Man Godfrey; *the result was one of the Thirties' funniest and most sophisticated screwball comedies (Universal, 1936).*

The refrigerator is empty, so why is Asta grinning? William Powell and Myrna Loy look more concerned; perhaps they are out of ice for the martinis. A scene from After The Thin Man *(MGM, 1936).*

The year in which Lombard made *Twentieth Century* – 1934 – was something of a vintage year for comedy, since *The Thin Man* and *It Happened One Night* were also released then.

The Thin Man was a detective story, and a highly competent one, adapted from a novel by Dashiell Hammett, but it was also a wonderfully warm, funny and zany portrait of a marriage. William Powell was the clever, fast-living, debonair, amateur-detective husband and Mynra Loy

his rich, beautiful and independent-spirited wife. The film established well their relationship with each other: mature, wise-cracking and teasing, with an attitude of 'Line up the martinis and we'll match each other sip for sip' – an awful lot of drinking was done in *The Thin Man* and even the dog, Asta, needed an icebag held to his aching brow at one point.

It Happened One Night scooped the Oscar pool in 1934, winning Best Picture, Best Director (Frank Capra), Best Actor

(Clark Gable), Best Actress (Claudette Colbert) and Best Screenplay (Robert Riskin). Rather more down to earth and a bit more sentimental than *Twentieth Century* and *The Thin Man*, it was directed with a light hand by Capra, and had a fine swing to the dialogue. It tells of the encounter between a millionaire's daughter running away from home and a tough but good-hearted newspaperman, who meet on a bus travelling from Miami to New York, and are forced to spend a night together, Gable preserving Colbert's maidenly modesty by hanging a blanket as a 'wall of Jericho' between their beds. By the time the film ends, after various adventures and incidents, love and marriage have worked their charms and the two are together in a bedroom again, with 'the wall of Jericho' tumbling down. Both Colbert and Gable were to make many more comedy films in their long careers, Gable generally giving the impression of a good straight actor (rather than a comedy player) getting by on charm and good looks, and Colbert, however screwball the comedy, always managing to look slightly fluffy and kittenish.

Katharine Hepburn and Cary Grant, who could almost be called a comedy 'team' of the 1930s, starring as they did in three great films together, were quite different. Unlike Gable, Cary Grant was a gifted comedian with a great sense of timing, a superb delivery and follow-through for sharp dialogue, as well as a suave style. Nor could anyone call Katharine Hepburn kittenish: tigerish perhaps, strong-minded, rangy and even sporty-looking certainly, and with looks that depended on bone-structure, rather than a fluffy presentation.

Grant and Hepburn first met not in a comedy but in *Sylvia Scarlett* (1935), taken from a Compton Mackenzie novel, and came together again in 1938 for two of the best of the Thirties screwball comedies, *Holiday* and *Bringing Up Baby*.

Clark Gable bares his chest, but Claudette Colbert looks less than captivated – so far – in It Happened One Night. *Director Frank Capra won the first of three Oscars he would collect in five years for this delightful movie (Columbia, 1934).*

Is the leopard Baby or a bad-tempered circus escapee? A fraught moment for Katharine Hepburn and Cary Grant in Bringing Up Baby *(RKO, 1938).*

In the latter, 'Baby' was a leopard that could be kept under control only by frequent doses of the song 'I Can't Give You Anything but Love, Baby'; Grant was David Huxley, a fussy professor of palaeontology needing one last 'intercostal clavicle' bone to complete his dinosaur before going off to marry a very upper-class and stern young woman; and Hepburn was also an upper-class, but very scatty and talkative young lady called Susan. Then there were Susan's aunt's dog, who stole the intercostal clavical and might have buried it in a twenty-acre garden in Connecticut; another (savage) leopard; a timid big-game hunter; an Irish groom (Barry Fitzgerald) usually the worse for drink; and Susan's millionairess aunt, played by the splendid May Robson. Together they take part in a Keystone-like chase. The ostensible chase is for lost leopards and a brontosaurus bone; the *real* chase is Susan's for David and she wins him from his frigid fiancée in the

end. Holding this brilliantly together and at the same time allowing it to run free in fine slapstick style was Howard Hawks, who had also directed *Twentieth Century*.

Holiday was a sophisticated comedy based on a play by Philip Barry first produced in the late Twenties, the theme of which – the pursuit of freedom, unfettered by social restraints – had grown out of Jazz Age attitudes. By the late Thirties, it was still relevant, particularly as it related to the place of women in society. Katharine Hepburn's wonderful performances in this and *Bringing Up Baby* not only did much to restore her sagging movie career but also emphasized the point that females could be lead stars in their own right, not just partners or sidekicks to the men whose names were above the title.

Hepburn and Grant were reunited in 1940 for the film ersion of another Philip Barry play, *The Philadelphia Story*. Hepburn had played the lead in the play on

Broadway, and had very cleverly bought the film rights. She sold them to MGM for no little profit, insisting on Cary Grant and James Stewart as the two male leads, and George Cukor as director. She certainly knew what she was doing. The film was an enormous popular success, and got her a third Academy Award Best Actress nomination. She lost to Ginger Rogers' performance in *Kitty Foyle* but found some compensation in a New York Film Critics' Award. James Stewart did win the Best Actor award for his performance in the film, in which he played the left-wing novelist-cum-journalist Macaulay Connor, sent by *Spy* magazine to cover the society wedding, who thinks he has fallen in love with the bride, Tracy Lord (Hepburn).

As the rather feeble 1950s re-make, *High Society*, showed, *The Philadelphia Story* could not have been made after the 1930s, the last era in which the upper-class rich could live as though wealth was

a natural state in which to exist, needing no defence on social or moral grounds. It was the sort of society in which a girl, embarking on what was, after all, her second marriage, could still expect to receive such wedding gifts as silver muffin dishes and wine coolers by the table-load, where there was always hot food in silver chafing-dishes for breakfast, and a swimming pool ready-made for midnight swims. To quote James Stewart in the film: 'The finest sight in this fine pretty world is the privileged class enjoying its privileges.'

If Cary Grant gave a deliciously urbane, tolerant and charming performance as Tracy's ex-husband, C. Dexter Haven who, of course, won her again as the final credits rolled, it was perhaps only to be expected. He had spent much of the late Thirties polishing his style in such films as *Topper* and *The Awful Truth*.

Topper (1937) is a ghost story, with Grant and Constance Bennett playing the

James Stewart becoming too involved with Katharine Hepburn in The Philadelphia Story. *Ruth Hussey looks concerned, but Cary Grant remains amazingly detached (MGM, 1940).*

ectoplasmic George and Marian Kirby, killed in a car accident and now needing to do a good deed on earth in order to win a place in heaven. They decide to direct their attentions towards stuffy Cosmo Topper (played here, and in the two follow-ups, by Roland Young), who needs freeing from the restraints of the boring business of banking to be allowed to discover the world and the life in it. After all, as the Kirbys have discovered, 'You can't take it with you.' Having ghosts in the story allowed for some fine visual gags. Is Topper keeping a woman in his hotel-room, or is he not? First the house detective sees her, then he doesn't. And how can the bellboy do his job when his guests are there one second and not the next? It was a theme that had worked well for René Clair two years before in his version of Robert Sherwood's fantasy comedy, *The Ghost Goes West*, though this film had rather lapsed into sentiment, which *Topper*, with its crisply written, sophisticated script, never did.

Grant starred with the elegant and aristocratic-looking Irene Dunne in *The Awful Truth* (1937), another of those 'crazy' comedies that derived much of its fun from seeing dignified people doing mad and undignified things. In *His Girl Friday* (1940), a version of the Hecht and MacArthur black comedy play, 'The Front Page', directed by Howard Hawks, Grant had as his partner Rosalind Russell, just beginning to work out the crisply suited, wise-cracking career woman character that would see her through the Forties. This was a newspaper story, with Grant as the editor Walter Burns and Russell as his ex-wife and keen young reporter Hildy Johnson (Hildy was a man in the original stage play, and in the other film version of it). Its plot was basically unpleasant, and not the usual stuff of comedy: newspapermen and town hall officials are gathered together like carrion crows to be in at the execution, or perhaps the reprieve, of a meek little man who has accidentally shot a policeman, and it is soon obvious that if there is to be a reprieve it will be for political motives, not because the judicial case warrants it. But Howard Hawks had a scintillating

It's the ghosts of Cary Grant and Constance Bennett playing about in Topper. *While Roland Young is just about coping, it is obviously all too much for his secretary (MGM/Hal Roach, 1937).*

cast and a script honed to splinter-sharp directness, and he set the whole thing at a fine old pace in which not a foot of film was wasted in unnecessary word or action.

As a director, Howard Hawks habitually took things at a fair speed, whether he was directing a western, a crime film or a comedy. His films were compactly made, and he was a master at editing them into a satisfying whole. He was not much concerned, though, with background frills, expensive settings or fancy camera angles, and as such, he makes a strong contrast with the German-born Ernst Lubitsch, who came to the United States in the 1920s and made some of the finest satirical comedies of sex and society, both silent and talkies, to come out of Hollywood, giving them the sparkling, frothy old-world sophistication and technical brillance that came to be known as 'the Lubitsch touch.' His sound output in the Twenties, Thirties and Forties included such stylish classics as *The Love Parade* (1929), *Trouble in Paradise* (1932), *Bluebeard's Eighth Wife* (1938), *Ninotchka* (1939) – in which, as everyone knows, Garbo laughed – and during the war years *To Be or Not to Be* (1942) and *Heaven Can Wait* (1943).

In His Girl Friday *there's a headline-grabbing story to be written, and editor Cary Grant is making sure that ace reporter Rosalind Russell is around to write it. Her fiancé Ralph Bellamy wishes she'd just come away and get married (Columbia, 1940).*

Jack Benny, leading a troupe of Shakespearian actors fleeing the Nazis, impersonated both Hamlet and Hitler in Lubitsch's To Be Or Not To Be. *Carole Lombard played the great actor's wife (Ernst Lubitsch, 1942).*

For Lubitsch, morality, 'correct' behaviour and social rights and wrongs hardly existed. His characters were not judged in terms of whether what they did was good or evil; rather he saw his characters in terms of conflicting emotions, desires and needs. It was an amoral, even cynical view of the world, made all the more startling by its contrast with the Viennese operetta-like frivolity of the settings in which he usually placed his stories.

Lubitsch's view of life was very much that of the cultured middle-European intellectual, honed to a cynical sophistication by experience. Perhaps the reason for the success of that other major director of comedy films of the Thirties, Frank Capra, whose films displayed such a different view of life, can be traced to *his* origins, which were southern European. Capra was of southern Italian, Catholic stock, having been born in Palermo, Sicily, and brought to the United States as a child. He was one of seven children

whom his peasant-stock father brought up via a precarious living picking oranges in California. There was no money in the Capra family for a fine intellectual education, and Frank had to make his own way, eventually graduating from university as a chemical engineer.

After war service and a period bumming around picking up jobs where he could, Capra talked his way into filmmaking in the 1920s, learning the job with such master craftsmen as Mack Sennett and Hal Roach, working as a gag writer for both of them. Perhaps instinctively he knew that comedy was to be his forte.

After his work with Harry Langdon and a shaky start as a director, Capra emerged in the Thirties as one of the best comedy directors of the day, his first big success being *It Happened One Night*. Capra was rather a sentimental idealist, believing in the essential ability of the good man to win out over the forces of darkness – usually in the form of big business and/or political corruption. They were themes Capra had first explored in the stories he had created for Langdon in the Twenties, such as the little man versus the great conglomerate of the Burton Shoe Company in *Tramp Tramp Tramp*.

By the Thirties, the over-weening conglomerate in the Capra comedies had become the big city, or even Washington itself. Both *Mr Deeds Goes to Town* (1936), which won Capra an Academy Award for Best Director, and *Mr Smith Goes to Washington* (1939) had an idealistic, if naïve young man, played by Gary Cooper and James Stewart respectively, coming to the big city to give the cynical, smooth-faced, immoral men in charge lesson in how goodness will triumph in the end. Looked at dispassionately, Capra's films were rose-tinted fairy stories but given a heart-warming conviction by his skills as a director, for he could film his scenes from exactly the right angle, for precisely the right length of time, and at

Longfellow Deeds (Gary Cooper) was a happy, tuba-playing fellow until he inherited a million dollars and things turned sour for him among the crooks of big business. Here, Jean Arthur commiserates with him in Mr Deeds Goes To Town *(Columbia, 1936).*

just the right pace to ensure that his audiences would get the message in his way, see what he wanted them to see.

His sentimental, Italian-immigrant gratitude for the best that existed in middle-class America was seen at its most amusing in the family comedy, *You Can't Take It with You*, which won the Oscars for Best Picture and Best Director in 1938. This was a sentimentalized, though not overly so, version of the highly successful George S. Kaufman-Moss Hart Broadway play, and starred James Stewart, with Jean Arthur, Lionel Barrymore, and numerous other Hollywood stalwarts.

While the films of Frank Capra, with their clever blend of tautly directed sentiment and sophistication, were among the best of the 'folksy' branch of 1930s American film comedy, they were not without rivals in the popularity stakes: the curly-headed, twinkle-toed infant, Shirley Temple, and the homespun, pleasant-faced Will Rogers offered some serious competition.

Will Rogers, who made no claims for his own abilities as an actor, appeared in more than sixty films, both silent and sound, before his untimely death in an air crash in 1935. He was apparently modest enough to believe that all the fan mail he received in the 1930s was simply a sign that the Great Depression was past its worst – people could afford stamps again. He seemed also to take little regard of the fact that at this time he was also the century's most popular box-office star. Probably he was too astute to think that fame was at best anything other than a shallow, short-lived thing. After all, he had been an entertainer since his teens, beginning in a Wild West show in South Africa during the Boer War, and had known many periods of decline. For instance, he had not been a great success in silent films since his personality was best expressed in words, not in acting, and most of his two-reel shorts for Hal Roach were not, as far as can be judged from those that survive, very original.

Frank Capra's splendid Mr Smith Goes to Washington *explored a favourite theme – the ordinary man against the machinations of politics and big business (Columbia, 1939).*

The advent of sound brought Will Rogers back to Hollywood from the stage, for which he had abandoned movies in the mid-Twenties. His first sound feature, *They Had to See Paris* (1929), directed by Frank Borzage, was an immediate success, with Rogers' unaffected, home spun charm and simple emotional responses coming across to audiences as the genuine expression of a warm and pleasing personality. The film was made for and released by Fox, under a one-picture contract, and they were so pleased with the success of this story of a suddenly wealthy Oklahoma family learning about life and love in Paris that they signed Rogers to a long-term contract under which he made another twenty features for them before his death, the last two being released posthumously.

Rogers' own strong personality and his disarming refusal to accept the conventions of film-making – he disliked repeating scenes and never bothered to learn his lines properly so that fluffed words, missed cues and dries were all likely to turn up in finished films, along with the occasional ad lib direct to camera – ensured that he was not an easy man to create films for. His best ones were those, like *Ambassador Bill* and *A Connecticut Yankee at the Court of King Arthur* (both 1931), *Doctor Bull* (1933), and *Judge Priest* (1934), in which he was allowed to display his own character within the limits of a not-too-heavy plot designed to be a

Will Rogers shares a pleasant moment or two with Fifi D'Orsay in Young as You Feel *(Fox, 1931).*

In the poster:
Shirley
TEMPLE
IN
The Poor Little
Rich Girl

ALICE FAYE GLORIA STUART
JACK HALEY MICHAEL WHALEN

Shirley Temple's twinkling toes and bobbing curls displayed in Poor Little Rich Girl *captivated audiences all over the world (Twentieth Century-Fox, 1936).*

good background for Rogers' special brand of crackerbarrel philosophy. Both *Doctor Bull* and *Judge Priest* were pictures of small-town America, with Will Rogers displaying a decent firmness of purpose against the forces of small-minded bureaucracy and over-blown ambition, and both were directed by John Ford, whose own deep and rather sentimental love of the America of ordinary folk may have appealed to Rogers, for in these films he was inspired to give what many critics consider his best performances.

Shirley Temple's place in the history of comedy in the movies rests primarily on the amount of genuine amusement that can be derived from a combination of sentiment, singing, dancing and an often cloyingly sweet cuteness, all of which constituted her pictures. More than just a child actress, she was the greatest phenomenon of the Depression-hit 1930s, a

particularly bright star in the cloudy sky to which people – or at least mothers with daughters – responded on a scale never known before or since. A huge industry producing Shirley Temple clothes, dolls, colouring books, paper cut-outs, storybooks and so on grew up almost overnight to feed the Shirley Temple cult that began after she was seen singing and dancing 'Baby Take a Bow' in *Stand Up and Cheer* in 1934, when she was six years old.

Most of her films – such as *Bright Eyes* (1934), *The Little Colonel* (1935) and *Captain January* (1936) – were a mixture of musical interludes and sentimental comedy of the kind that produces a smile and a chuckle rather than a loud laugh. The best of the dancing was in *The Little Colonel* and *The Littlest Rebel* (both 1935) because she was partnered with Bill 'Bojangles' Robinson, a dancer of considerable natural charm. Perhaps the main point of the Shirley Temple films is that they provided the route by which sentiment gradually replaced screwball sophistication in the comedy films of the 1930s.

The Andy Hardy films, which were a sort of trading post on the route from 1930s comedy to the quite different comedy of the post-war 1940s, were about adolescents, rather than children, and had distinctly thin and rather silly story-lines within a 'nice' middle-class family setting where Father was a judge and Mother was, well, motherly. Mickey Rooney, from a vaudeville family and with an early start in the family act at the age of about fifteen months, played the cocky Andy Hardy. The first film in what became a 'B' picture series was *A Family Affair* (1937), and was followed by fourteen more Andy Hardy films over the next ten years. By 1939, Mickey Rooney had toppled Shirley Temple from her place at the apex of the box-office popularity tree, having in 1938 shared with Deanna Durbin a special Academy Award for their significant contribution in bringing 'the spirit and personification of youth' to the screen.

The Andy Hardy films were all reassuringly sentimental, warmly extolling the virtues of the simple life enjoyed by good-living families in which the worst thing that could happen would be Andy having girl trouble (in the nicest, most innocent possible way).

The films were enormously popular in America and abroad, mainly because, for part of the series, they were portraying the peace and tranquillity of family life during a period of war and suffering; they seemed to be suggesting that once the

Judge Hardy and Son was the eighth in the 'Andy Hardy' series. Involved in the washing up are the judge, Lewis Stone, his son Andy, Mickey Rooney, and Cecilia Parker, Sara Haden and Fay Holden (MGM, 1939).

Wide Open Faces – *an appropriate title for a Joe E Brown vehicle. (Columbia, 1938).*

war was over and Hitler out of the way, there would still be the simple virtues of life to return to.

In this chapter, we have skimmed the cream off the top of the comedy output of the first decade or so of the talkies era. Countless minor comedies were made in the 1930s, many of them being used to fill part of the double bill that became a standard draw in cinemas everywhere, and the actors in them often never made it into the major league of films, those that monopolize the attention of film buffs and historians. How many of us, for instance, could put a face to the name Franklin Pangborn? Yet he appeared in about seventy movies in the Thirties and Forties, including W. C. Fields' *The Bank Dick* in which he was J. Pinkerton Snoopington. Then there was the delightfully jittery Edward Everett Horton, who played comedy leads and character roles in something like 150 films from the Twenties right

through to the early Seventies (remember him as Fred Astaire's friend and sidekick in *Top Hat*?).

Joe E. Brown was rather different. He was a minor-league comic player, though he made several good comedies in the 1930s, including *Elmer the Great* (1933) and *Alibi Ike* (1935), and he played Flute in the Max Reinhardt-William Dieterle production of *A Midsummer Night's Dream*, in which Mickey Rooney was Puck. Most of us *can* remember his face, with its wide, lemon-slice smile, but probably more for his Cap'n Andy in the Howard Keel-Kathryn Grayson *Showboat* (1951) and his superb tango-dancing Osgood Fielding in Billy Wilder's *Some Like It Hot* (1959) than for anything he did in the 1930s.

To Joe, and to the countless others, unnamed here, who helped make the 1930s the greatest period in movie comedy – thanks for the memory!

80

MONKEY BUSINESS:
THE GREAT MOVIE TEAMS

Most actors would agree that it is probably easier to get to the top of their profession as a solo performer than as part of a team: an actor can 'do his own thing' and also be seen to be doing it – he is not looked on as just one part of a group. Even so, in the great days of film comedy, it was the teams who provided the cinema with some of its funniest and most enduring moments. The great solo performers – Chaplin, Keaton, Lloyd and Langdon at their best – tended to be great in visual terms, but when the comedy came to have words – wisecracks, jokes, witty repartee – as its essential element, then team acting came to the fore. For example, Cary Grant and Katharine Hepburn were fine solo actors, but together they became a team because, in their films, the dialogue spoken by one could only be effective if it bounced off or was responded to by the other.

While actors such as Grant and Hepburn and Powell and Loy became teams only for the duration of specific films, the great comedy teams of the Thirties and Forties chose to stay together because they did their best work when the quite distinct characters of each member were interrelating and sparking off each other. The two greatest comedy teams hardly worked at all as solo artists.

Of the four Marx Brothers, the only one to make any mark by going solo was Groucho, and he, though he was not the eldest, always seemed the leader of the pack anyway. Laurel and Hardy started out as solo performers, but achieved greatness as a team and when Oliver Hardy died after a stroke, Stan Laurel did not make another film.

Even so, as the career of the Abbott and Costello duo shows, teamwork alone does not make for movie comedy greatness. It is not enough to have been a success in burlesque, on Broadway, on radio or even, for that matter, on television. There has to be an extra dimension, an awareness, conscious or not, on the part of each member of the team that comedy performed on the big screen is not the same thing as live comedy.

Although Abbott and Costello were successful enough in translating their stage and radio *personae* and routines to the screen, they never took much interest in how the technicalities and conventions of film-making – the inter-relationship between actor, camera and screen – could be used to create a type of comedy totally different from that of live performances. To achieve a mastery of the movie comedy form, dialogue on its own, however funny, witty or clever, is not enough, as was to be proved many times.

It is this same problem that keeps the very funny vaudeville, radio and television partnership of George Burns and Gracie Allen out of any list of great movie comedy teams. They actually appeared in a good number of films, including *We're Not Dressing* and *Six of a Kind* (both 1934) and *Damsel in Distress* (1937), in which they provided many amusing moments, but they were the same kind of moments that Burns and Allen gave their stage and radio audiences: they were great comedians but not completely in control of the movie comedy form. It is, however, a nice little irony of movie history that George Burns had to wait over thirty years and to go solo before he achieved positive recognition of his abilities as a film actor. In 1975, he won an Oscar for Best Supporting Actor for his part in Neil Simon's *The Sunshine Boys*.

The Marx Brothers

The Marx Brothers came to the movies via vaudeville and the Broadway stage, and they had been more or less raised for that by their mother, Minnie, a daughter and sister of show-business folk. The brothers' early years in vaudeville were as part of numerous musical acts, in which there would be variously two, three or four of Minnie's five sons at any one time, but it was not until they switched from music to comedy acts that their careers began to take off, though it was a desperately slow and ill-paid business at first.

By the mid-Twenties, they had made it to Broadway where, in such musical comedy shows as 'I'll Say She Is' (1924), 'The Cocoanuts' (1925) and 'Animal Crackers' (1928), they really began to gel as a team, developing a style that was quite inimitable as well as personal characters that were also unique. Even within the disciplined confines of a Broadway show, they would ad lib their way through scenes, creating havoc and shortening the lives of other actors. The Marx Brothers' business was pure comedy – comedy for its own sake, with no attempt or desire to make it a vehicle for social comment, political proselytizing or satire, though social destruction and the puncturing of pomposity figured largely in their work.

Groucho (real name Julius Henry), though the third-born of the brothers, was the leader. He was the one with the extraordinary bent-knee gait, the (at first) painted on moustache, the heavy eyebrows running up and down like semaphore signals behind the steel-rimmed glasses he affected, and the large cigar. He was also the talker of the group, with a non-stop flow of words delivered like bullets from a machine gun, and just as unstoppable.

Harpo (Adolph, usually called Arthur) was the mute with the blonde curly hair, child-like smile, satyr-like lecherous eye for a pretty girl, and too-big trousers and coat, from the recesses of which he could be relied on to produce some prop that would help his speechless pantomime 'talking' – a swordfish if he needed to get into a speakeasy where the password was 'Swordfish', a phonograph record to which he could mime a Maurice Chevalier song or, very often, an old car horn whose beeps and hoots could help signify whole sentences. He could also play the harp.

Chico (Leonard) was the oldest Marx brother and the one best able to interpret Harpo's 'speech' to the rest of the world, particularly Groucho. Chico was the pianist of the team and spoke his crazy punladen English with a strong Italian accent.

Zeppo (Herbert), the conventional Marx brother, was the one who never got mixed up in their mad goings on, but tended to hang about on the sidelines looking bland in rather boring 'romantic' parts, both in their Broadway shows and in their first five films, after which he dropped out of the lunatic, anarchic world to become an agent.

The four Marx Brothers, who had had only little experience of the movie business (in a silent film called *Humour Risk*, which was not completed), were invited to take a bigger step into the world of the cinema quite soon after the introduction of sound. The talent scouts at Paramount Studios saw the potential for film comedy in the crazy Broadway clowns, and the studio put them in front of the cameras to recreate two of their Broadway successes in *The Cocoanuts* (1929) and *Animal Crackers* (1930). Both films were made at Paramount's Astoria studios on Long Island, so that the brothers could film during the day and act on stage at night. These early movies were terribly stagebound, cluttered up with 'romantic' male singers and musical 'interludes', and directed in a very ham-fisted style, but even so, the Marx Brothers' talent showed through it all, and more than one film critic saw that here were clowns of great potential.

Appearing in both the films was the wonderfully handsome and statuesque Margaret Dumont, who had had a baptism of fire, as it were, by appearing with them in their stage comedies. She would act in another five Marx Brothers' comedies, creating with Groucho a classic screen couple.

After *Animal Crackers*, the Marx Brothers went west, to make films on Paramount's Hollywood lot. The studio more or less allowed them to create their own style, though Paramount were interested enough to assign some really good writers to their films. The result was three of the wildest, most anarchic comedies ever made in Hollywood: *Monkey Business* (1931), *Horse Feathers* (1932) and *Duck Soup* (1933).

Paramount's
All Talking-Singing
MUSICAL COMEDY HIT!

The MARX BROTHERS

THE Cocoanuts IN

WITH

OSCAR SHAW and MARY EATON

*The Marx Brothers –
Groucho, Harpo,
Chico and Zeppo –
wear natty boaters to
stand out from the
crowd in this scene
from* Monkey Business
(Paramount, 1931).

Monkey Business was, for anyone who could sort it out, a story of a gangster feud, with a shipboard romance thrown in. Groucho was a con-man intent on becoming as intimate as possible with the wife of the tough gangster and society nob, Alky Briggs. Thelma Todd played the wife, and as the film progressed, Groucho's advances became more and more marked. 'Mrs. Briggs,' he said, 'I've known and respected your husband Alky for many years, and what's good enough for him is good enough for me,' and, so saying, he jumps on her lap. Eventually, the two dance a tango on the bed in Mrs. Briggs' shipboard stateroom.

The anarchy in *Monkey Business* involved numerous breathless chases, including one where the four Marx Brothers as stowaways are chased by the ship's captain and crew. Harpo ends up hiding inside a puppet theatre while the

children on board are being given a show, and every so often, his wide-eyed childish face appears among the scenery.

Horse Feathers had a screenplay by (among others) the famous comic writer S. J. Perelman and the songwriters Bert Kalmar and Harry Ruby, who provided a tighter script than usual for this 'simple' tale of college life, in which Groucho was Professor Wagstaff, head of Huxley College, and Zeppo was his son Frank. There was also a girl (Thelma Todd) whom both the Professor and Frank fancied. (Typical Marxian pun: Professor to the girl, discovered sitting on Frank's knee: 'Young lady, would you get up so that I can see the son rise?')

While *Horse Feathers* was funnier than most other comedies of the time, it was not entirely effective. The film was very much Groucho's, with not a lot for Harpo and Chico to do; as a result their comic routines did not rise above the ordinary.

This criticism could not be levelled at the wonderfully structured and hilariously funny *Duck Soup*. Once again, Bert Kalmar and Harry Ruby were in charge of the script, and the direction was in the experienced hands of the fine comedy director Leo McCarey, who worked with most of the great comedy players of the Twenties and Thirties, including Charlie Chase, Laurel and Hardy, Eddie Cantor, Mae West, W. C. Fields and Harold Lloyd, and who later won Oscars for *The Awful Truth* and *Going My Way*.

Together, this more than merely talented team produced the most satisfying Marx Brothers' film – and many people's favourite – and the one that,

together with their first for MGM, *A Night at the Opera* (1935), shows the Marx Brothers at their best. It is all the more astonishing, then, to discover that *Duck Soup* was not a box office success in 1933 and was to mark the end of the Marx Brothers' association with Paramount.

Duck Soup was about politics and war, but with a view that was insanely anarchic and nothing like the ordered attack on the subject made by Chaplin in *Shoulder Arms*. Margaret Dumont was back in the picture as Groucho's leading lady, the immensely rich Mrs. Teasdale, who is prepared to bale her country, Freedonia, out of its bankrupt state if it will appoint the great Rufus T. Firefly (Groucho) as its

Thelma Todd may have trouble rescuing that ankle from the attentions of a lecherous Harpo: a mad moment from Horse Feathers *(Paramount, 1932).*

president. It does, and the inevitable result is chaos all round, with President Firefly being so insulting to the Sylvanian ambassador that the two countries end up at war.

Harpo and Chico figured as spies, though Harpo spent too much time cutting ties, coat tails and cigar ends off anyone he could get his scissors near to be very effective in his guise. Their best visual gags – and in *Duck Soup* these were great indeed – had nothing to do with the plot. There was a hugely funny hat routine with a lemonade salesman played by Arthur Kennedy, and a classic mirror gag, first used by the great Max Linder, in which Chico and Harpo try to hide from Groucho the fact that they have broken his floor-length looking-glass: first, Harpo dresses the same as Groucho, in nightshirt and cap, cigar and glasses, and copies the latter's movements in front of the mirror so perfectly that Groucho does not notice anything wrong; then Chico, similarly dressed, appears and wrecks the deception, President Firefly not being silly enough to think that there are two of him.

Duck Soup reached a side-splitting climax in the great war sequence that united sound and visual gags in super-abundance. As President Firefly marches back and forth across the floor at his battle headquarters, his uniform changes style

The true Marx Brothers anarchic spirit gets free rein in this scene from A Day at the Races *(MGM, 1937).*

Salute to a gracious lady: Sig Ruman plants one on Margaret Dumont's be-jewelled hand in A Night at the Opera *while Groucho fakes a masterly disinterest (MGM, 1935).*

until in the end he looks like Daniel Boone. Harpo, chosen by Chico's dubious Eeny, meeny, miny mo' routine to carry a message asking for reinforcements across the battlefield, is sent off by President Firefly with the uplifting thought that 'You are a brave man. Remember, when you are out there risking your life and limb, through shot and shell, we'll be in here thinking what a sucker you are.'

Mrs. Teasdale arrives to offer moral support, so the President sends his troops into battle with the unusual speech 'Remember, men, you're fighting for this woman's honour – which is probably more than she ever did.'

After this anarchic comedy was launched in America to less than total success and Paramount began to think again about employing the Marx Brothers, Chico found himself playing cards with the great man of Metro-Goldwyn-Mayer, Irving Thalberg. Thalberg felt that the Marx Brothers' movies

needed better production values, and who better to provide them than MGM? So, a deal was done, and the Marx Brothers, except Zeppo who now bowed out, moved to MGM, where their best period encompassed the splendid *A Night at the Opera* and *A Day at the Races* (1937), and where even the less successful (because less sharp and too hedged about by MGM flossiness and sugary romantic comedy) *At the Circus* (1939), *Go West* (1940) and *The Big Store* (1941) provided many happy instances of the Marxian comedy's unique style.

A Night at the Opera had Groucho as Otis B. Driftwood, a would-be opera singers' agent ('You're willing to pay him a thousand bucks a night just for singing? You can get a phonograph record of "Minnie the Moocher" for seventy-five cents. For a buck and a quarter you can get Minnie.'), and Margaret Dumont as Mrs. Claypool, a lady hoping that Driftwood has the necessary clout to introduce

GROUCHO · CHICO · HARPO

MARX BROS.

GO WEST

A Metro-Goldwyn-Mayer PICTURE

RIP-ROARING WITH LAUGHS, GIRLS, SONGS!

John CARROLL
Diana LEWIS

Original Screen Play by IRVING BRECHER
Directed by EDWARD BUZZELL · Produced by JACK CUMMINGS

The Marx Brothers had long been a threesome by the time they came to make Go West *(MGM, 1940).*

her into society. The film also contained the famous gag involving a tiny shipboard cabin full of people, including the Marx Brothers, Allan Jones, a stewardess or two and a lady looking for her Aunt Minnie, with Groucho's voice, rising over all, crying at regular intervals: 'Make that three hard-boiled eggs.' And there was the contract gag, with 'The party of the first party...' and the sanity clause about which Chico makes his immortal remark: 'Ha, ha, you can't-a fool me. There ain't no Sanity Claus.'

A Day at the Races was set variously at a race track and in a sanitarium, where one of the more memorable scenes had the Marx Brothers as bogus doctors, led by Groucho as Dr. Hugo Z. Hackenbush, examining Margaret Dumont as if she were a car in need of new parts. This was also the film in which Chico did his great 'tutsi-frutsi ice-cream-a' salesman routine.

The Marx Brothers' best film after this was the independently made *A Night in*

Casablanca (1945), which looked a bit cheap, but still contained some good jokes, and a very fruity part for Groucho as Ronald Kornblow, a hotel manager with an amazingly off-hand way with his guests:

GUEST: Sir, this lady is my wife. You should be ashamed.
KORNBLOW: If this lady is your wife, you should be ashamed.
GUEST: You'll hear from me, sir!
KORNBLOW: Do that, even if it's only a postcard.

After this came the poor *Love Happy* (1950), notable today only for an early appearance by Marilyn Monroe as a curvaceous blonde with a problem – 'Men keep following me all the time' – and after this, the Marx Brothers did not make another film together. Still, they had had a long run together, and their consistent performances as a comic team are never likely to be equalled.

Laurel and Hardy

As it had done for so many comedians in the early decades of the movies, the vaudeville theatre provided the training ground for both the English-born Stanley Laurel and the American Oliver Hardy.

Stan was born in 1890, and joined the Fred Karno troupe when he was twenty, being made Chaplin's understudy for Karno's first American tour in 1910. At the end of the Karno company's second trip to the United States, in 1912, Stan Laurel stayed on to try his luck in American vaudeville, and was in fairly constant employment from then on. Even when he tried film acting in 1917 when he appeared in the two-reel shorts, *Nuts in May* and *Lucky Dog*, the latter also having one Oliver Hardy among the bit players, he retained a footing in vaudeville.

For some years, he did both, freelancing with a number of film companies both as actor and writer, and appearing in over 40

Ollie and Stan contemplate far horizons in Sons of the Desert *(MGM/Hal Roach, 1933).*

The opening shots in the silent classic tit-for-tat, Laurel and Hardy versus James Finlayson, battle in Big Business *(Pathé/Hal Roach, 1929).*

shorts between 1917 and 1926; he even did some directing. It was not until 1926 that, having signed a contract to write and direct for Hal Roach, he was persuaded to appear on screen too, with a fat actor whose appearance might contrast well with his own skinniness in comedy sketches. So, Laurel and Oliver Hardy made *Forty-five Minutes from Hollywood* together, and the teaming was to last almost twenty five years.

Hardy, two years younger than Laurel, was born in Georgia and began singing with a minstrel show when he was eight – presumably with the blessing of his lawyer father. Even though he went to the University of Georgia to study law, it was obvious that the call of drama was too strong to be ignored, and by 1910 Hardy had opened a small movie house. In 1913 he joined the Lubin film company where, rotund even then, he was generally given comic villain parts.

He was never much more than a second-string character actor until the fateful year when he was teamed up with Laurel by director Leo McCarey for a series of slapstick shorts. A couple of decades later, they would be able to look back on a career that had made them known and loved throughout the world – probably the most successful and best-loved comedy duo the film world will ever know.

Their style, worked out mostly through the ideas and writing of Stan Laurel, since Ollie Hardy was never much of an ideas man, was a gentle, almost child-like one. Not for Stan and Ollie the combination of sophisticated satire, lechery and plain rudeness in distinctly dubious taste that characterized much of the Marx Brothers' output. The Laurel and Hardy brand of slapstick was kinder, and therefore appealed to a wider audience, to adults and children alike.

It was also slower, more deliberate and without the frenzy that generally characterized slapstick. Take the famous tit-for-tat wrecking sequence in the silent short, *Big Business* (1929): it was Laurel and Hardy versus Jimmy Finlayson, with the two systematically wrecking Finlayson's house – here a garden plant, there a door, then a window, attacked with an axe – and Finlayson reciprocating with an attack on their car for every attack on his house and person. It was all done very deliberately and in sequence, with one action completed and considered before the reciprocal one was begun, and made all the funnier thereby. In *The Battle of the Century* (1927), there may have been custard pies flying about in true slapstick style, but they were all thrown for a logical reason, and with a target in mind.

In all their films, Stan – 'the thin one' with a light-weight brain to match – was given to scratching his head when in doubt (which was often) and to bursting into tears when in trouble (which was also often). Ollie – the fat dignified one – was constantly exasperated and embarrassed by simple Stan's silliness. He was the one who, impatiently deciding to go ahead of Stan because the latter was so slow, would be hit by the falling object as he walked through the door, and he would react to each fall from dignity with a nervous twiddling of his tie. Most of his troubles he saw as being caused not by his own incompetence but by Stan's having got him into 'another fine mess'. However, we the audience know that both these fellows, however silly, must be respectable men because each wears a derby hat.

The world that these two simple characters inhabited was, as they saw it, an inherently good and reasonable one, a society in which, if things went wrong, they could believe that the wrongs had been their own fault, while the fortunate

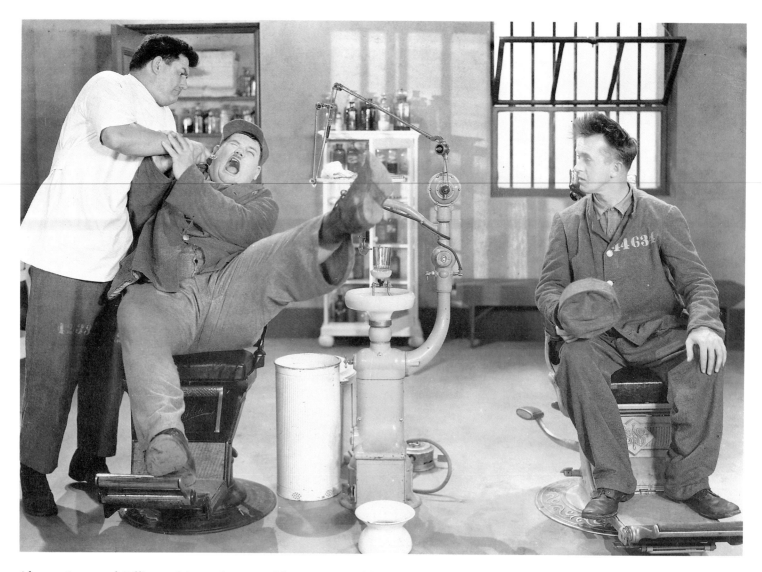

things they could see as good luck. It was a very appealing approach, made all the more so by the obvious empathy between the two men, and the warmth of the relationship between them: whatever happened, they were in it together. Thus, their comedy had a humanity not usually found in the generally two-dimensional world of slapstick. It was a plus, too, that both men were more than competent actors and that they both had good voices, so that when they made the jump from silent slapstick comedy to sound in 1929, they did so without difficulty and with no diminution in the quality of their characterizations or believability.

Together, Laurel and Hardy appeared in over 100 films, three-quarters of which were silent and sound shorts produced by Hal Roach. Most of these were based on single incidents that were carried through to their logical conclusion, and all were rooted in everyday reality, in situations with which their audiences could identify. For instance, the near-perfect short, *The Music Box*, for which they won an Oscar

in 1932, was about getting a piano up a flight of steps to the house at the top. Among the hundred films were twenty-seven sound features of which *Pardon Us* (*Jailbirds* in UK), made in 1931 for Hal Roach/MGM, was the first in which they had starring, rather than guest or supporting, roles. Both this film and their next, *Pack Up Your Troubles* (1932), looked rather episodic, like a series of musical hall turns patched together, and it was not until they got to their sixth feature film, *Sons of the Desert* (*Fraternally Yours* in UK, 1933), that they showed they had at last thrown off the inhibitions that were a legacy of all those years making short, one-situation movies, and they produced something with a good plot-line that looked coherent and all of a piece.

In fact, *Sons of the Desert* is one of their best films, both technically and as a feature-length comedy, with a well-controlled relationship between story, characters and gags. Its story is basically simple: two men, trying to get away from

STAN **LAUREL** Oliver **HARDY** in **WAY OUT WEST**

A Metro-Goldwyn-Mayer PICTURE

Above: Laurel and Hardy did a soft shoe dance and sang 'On The Trail of the Lonesome Pine' in Way Out West (MGM/Hal Roach, 1937).

Right: Stan and Ollie pause for breath amid the chaos in Blockheads (MGM/ Hal Roach, 1938).

their wives for a time, attempt to deceive them with a story that Ollie's doctor has ordered him off to Hawaii for a rest cure. Where the two really head for is the convention of a Freemasons-like outfit called the 'Sons of the Desert' in Chicago (where there are some good moments with the veteran Charlie Chase). Returned home, the boys, still with the leis round their necks and ukeleles in their hands, which were to have added verisimilitude to the Hawaii story, discover that the ship on which they were supposed to have been travelling has been shipwrecked .... Another fine mess is clearly in sight.

Laurel and Hardy were at their peak with *Way Out West* (1937) – memorable for their dance routine in the main street of Brushwood Gulch and their singing of 'On The Trail of the Lonesome Pine' – and *Blockheads* (1938), in which kind-hearted Hardy attempts to help his homeless wartime buddy, Laurel, by inviting him to stay. Some of the gags in this were devised by Harry Langdon.

Blockheads would have been better if it had been Laurel and Hardy's last film, for after it, the duo's comedy declined. Their films began to be rather leaden-footed with too much dull material between the good bits, a problem already beginning to show in *A Chump at Oxford* and *Saps at Sea*, both of which were made in 1940 and marked the end of the pair's association with Hal Roach. Now there was no studio willing to put up the first-rate script writers and directors necessary to take them back to the top.

Their last film was the French/Italian co-production *Atoll K*, a disaster also known as *Robinson Crusoeland* and *Utopia*, which appeared in 1951. In the mid-1950s, Oliver Hardy suffered a severe stroke, from which he never recovered, dying in 1957. Stan Laurel carried on as a writer, working up to his death in 1965. In 1960 he had received a special Oscar for his 'creative pioneering in the field of cinema comedy'. It was well deserved, for at their best Laurel and Hardy had turned basic slapstick into something of much higher artistic merit and had given the world two warm and lovable characters to laugh with.

A relaxing moment between takes for one of movie comedy's greatest teams, Laurel and Hardy, and their producer, Hal Roach.

Abbott and Costello

While Laurel and Hardy's star was waning in the Forties, that of Abbott and Costello was rising, but it would always glow less brightly for, despite their enormous popularity in the Forties and Fifties, they were less skilled actors than Laurel and Hardy, and lacked their warmth and humanity. In particular, Bud Abbott was too much Lou Costello's straight man for the two to be seen as a real partnership of pals. Even so, a comedy pair whose second feature film, *Buck Privates* (*Rookies* in UK, 1941), grossed $10 million and who were consistently among the Top Ten box-office grossers throughout the

Forties cannot be left out of any consideration of the great teams of movie comedy.

Both men came to film from burlesque, where they had each over the years established specific characters that were easily recognizable by burlesque, Broadway and radio audiences. On the whole, they were to put these characters on to the screen unchanged, and relied heavily on their burlesque years for the material for their films: when that ran out and they offloaded their best writer, John Grant, the average Abbott and Costello movie became uninspired and pedestrian (to put it kindly). Even the successful *Buck Privates* had been little more than a series of

Buck Privates *was the first big hit for Bud Abbott and Lou Costello (Universal, 1941).*

"I'm caught in the washing machine... they're taking me to the cleaners!"

sketches and gags from their stage and radio acts, held together with some music and a mild love-story sub-plot.

The Abbott and Costello screen characters that were established in *Buck Privates* had Abbott as the rather cold, sharp straight man and Costello as the lovable, almost child-like little man. It was clear that the two men, as dialogue/patter comedians rather than action men, needed each other to provide the necessary bounce-back for their routines, but it was also apparent that as screen characters they did not have the warm feelings towards each other as had Laurel and Hardy: the Abbott character was all too often that of the con-man willing to sacrifice the Costello character in order to win advantages for himself. Even in action, they did not work too well together. Costello despite his roly-poly figure, was pretty agile, the legacy of a youth spent being a Hollywood stunt man, while Abbott was never a 'physical' actor.

Despite all these drawbacks, Bud Abbott and Lou Costello survived as a Hollywood movie comedy partnership for sixteen years, a reasonable record in itself, and did produce a few not too bad movies in that time. There was *The Time of Their Lives* (1946), for instance, a ghost story with a twist. Lou Costello and Marjorie Reynolds were an 18th-century New England couple whose ghosts had remained in their house ever since they had been framed in a conspiracy perpetrated by a man whose descendant is now, in the mid-1940s, planning to renovate and live in the old house. Bud Abbott was on hand as a psychiatrist friend of the man.

Abbott and Costello Meet Frankenstein (1948) was another of their movies with some great moments. In it, the pair get mixed up with some of the great men of movie horror – including Frankenstein, Count Dracula (Bela Lugosi himself) and the Wolfman (Lon Chaney, Jr.) – and the film worked because the horror was taken

Lou's in a twist, but Bud seems to be offering little help in Rio Rita (MGM, 1942).

straight and not lampooned as it might have been. There were plenty of genuine chills to scare audiences, and also some good jokes, like the one involving the moving candle that had first appeared in an early Abbott and Costello effort, *Hold That Ghost* (1941). This time, the candle was set on Count Dracula's coffin and moved every time the Count tried to sit up under the lid. Unfortunately, it was only Costello who saw the candle move; every time Abbott turned to look, the Count, and the candle, were still.

By the end of the Forties, the Abbott and Costello screen partnership was running out of steam. They had long since used up their best burlesque material and, since neither man made much more of a contribution to their films other than to act in them, they had to rely on other people to provide the raw material for them. Provided there were plenty of laughs to be had, they were not too worried that the movies had thin plots, little characterization and no consistent style running between their films.

Abbott and Costello split up after *Dance With Me, Henry* in 1956. Abbott did not appear again in films – apart from the compilation feature *The World of Abbott and Costello* that Universal, which had released most of their films, put out in 1965 – but Lou Costello made one film alone, *The Thirty-Foot Bride of Candy Rock*, in 1959, the year he died.

Today, their films, little regarded by critics, still pull in audiences on television, and their most famous routine, 'Who's on First?', a classic piece of dialogue that they included in *The Naughty Nineties* (1945), is now a favourite Abbott and Costello quote.

Lou Costello was an 18th-century ghost and Bud Abbott the friend of a 20th-century house owner, John Shelton (left), in The Time of Their Lives *(Universal, 1946).*

The Three Stooges

This was the team that, more often than not, would fill, along with the cartoon, travelogue, newsreel, etc., the first half of the programme before the feature film, from the beginning of the Thirties right through to the end of the Fifties. During these thirty years, the team made more than 200 shorts and feature films at Columbia, and nobody thought very much of their brash and violent form of clowning about until the shorts began to be shown on American television in the late Fifties and the kids loved them.

The team's name derived from the fact that for several years they were the on-stage foils, or 'stooges' for vaudeville comedian Ted Healy, and their first half-dozen shorts and feature films were all Ted Healy vehicles. When they launched out on their own in 1934, they kept the Stooges name. They remained two-dimensional clowns and their rather surreal slapstick meant that they did not seem to function as real human beings.

The composition of the team changed over the years – after all, they were in the business for over forty years. The original group of Moe Howard, Larry Fine and Shemp Howard appeared in their first feature film, *Soup to Nuts* (1930), in which they were listed as 'the Racketeers' and were little more than background figures behind Ted Healy, but then Shemp left the group and was replaced by his brother Curly, only to come back in the Forties when Curly had a stroke. There were also changes at the latter end of their career, when Shemp died and was replaced in the act first by Joe Besser and then by Joe De Rita, both of whom were professional comics from vaudeville.

In most of their films, The Three Stooges went in for a physically rough and even violent kind of slapstick, much of it being perpetrated by Moe – which is probably why the kids liked them so much. There was no subtlety about their comedy, which sometimes ended up on the wrong side of the barrier between acceptable and unacceptable violence.

At their best, though, they could provide a tightly controlled, and nicely improvised form of comedy, more than sufficient to while away the first part of the programme before the interval.

The Three Stooges were all in their sixties, but still pretty vigorous, when they made the feature film The Three Stooges Meet Hercules *(Columbia/Normandy Productions, 1962).*

99

WHAT A CARRY ON:
THE COMEDY FILM IN BRITAIN

Although comedy has been an important component of English drama from its earliest days, it did not play any major part in the films being made in Britain in the 1920s, a time when Chaplin, Keaton, Harry Langdon and others were making the immortal comic films that helped establish the American film industry as the world's biggest, the most popular and the richest.

In Britain, as elsewhere in Europe, prevailing attitudes among those with clout in the young film industry meant that much film comedy was dictated by middle-class beliefs and values and was all too often banal and sugary, full of innocuous plots and sentimental imagery of the kind found in *The Constant Nymph* (1928). The humour was generally derivative, coming straight from the vaudeville or West End matinée stage, or else mimicking Hollywood styles. Walter Forde, for instance, wore a boater and glasses in the Harold Lloyd manner, but turned Lloyd's distinctive, simple young American into figures that were more caricature than real, being a vapid English aristocrat or a smart-alec salesman, as occasion demanded.

An early attempt to produce good British screen comedy, but free of Hollywood 'vulgarity', was made by a company called Minerva Films, set up in 1920, with its directors including such talents as C. Aubrey Smith and Leslie Howard, both of whom would later find success in Hollywood as true personifications of English gentlemanliness. (Aubrey Smith even ran the Hollywood cricket club, and you could not become more quintessentially English than that.) It was Minerva's intention to produce comedy in 'good taste', and before its premature demise in a sea of financial troubles and a lack of audience interest, it did manage to produce some comedy films, including a few shorts written by A. A. Milne.

Alf's Button (1920) made by Cecil Hepworth, from a play by W. A. Darlington and starring the music-hall actor Leslie Henson, was a more successful feature comedy of the time. This tale of a magic button with properties akin to those of Aladdin's lamp had sufficient good taste to enable one reviewer to comment on its magnificent wit and the clever subtitles that, he noted, had none of the slang that spoiled American films for British audiences. The film was a big financial success for Hepworth but only a moderate success among audiences who, prepared to accept 'vulgarity' for the sake of 'vitality', were taking the impudent and iconoclastic American style of comedy to their collective bosom.

Unable to stand up to the American onslaught on British cinemas, the British film industry sought and was given protection by the government, which introduced the 'quota' system under which film imports were to be limited and a certain percentage of films shown in British cinemas would have to be of British origin. This protection, coinciding with the arrival of the American talkies — understandably rejected by film audiences temporarily when they first heard actors speaking slang in odd-sounding, strong nasal accents — gave a boost to British films, especially comedy, which was also helped by the fact that American spoken jokes lacked the universality of the silent gesture or facial expression of the silent comedian.

What was still lacking in Britain, however, was an approach to film as a

medium in its own right, and there was a continuing tendency to transport theatre comedy and its actors directly on to the screen without adapting them to the new medium. British comedy films of the 1930s featured the same names as were to be found on music-hall and theatre hoardings the length of the kingdom. Arthur Askey, Gracie Fields, Will Hay, Will Fyffe, Tommy Handley, Max Miller, the Crazy Gang and the Aldwych farce team of Tom Walls, Ralph Lynn, Claude Hulbert and Robertson Hare were all translated, their acts and personalities almost intact, on to the screen.

The Aldwych farces, many of them written by Ben Travers, were a kind of stage version of the world of P. G. Wodehouse. Tom Walls was the generally well-dressed, or at least well-off, representative of the upper middle classes while Ralph Lynn was the asinine aspect of the same class – a fool but a nicely brought-up and gentlemanly one and a character dear to the hearts of British audiences who generally regarded him with a fond patronage. Also always in the team was Robertson Hare, a small, bald, nervous little man who, in character, spoke with a stammer, as well he might for he was so obviously lower middle class – a tradesman, or lawyer's clerk, or a servant to the other two – always ill at ease but knowing his place in society and therefore acceptable.

The team's 'hero' was, more often than not, Ralph Lynn. He was with the team at the Aldwych theatre throughout the Twenties, who appeared in some of their best films in the 1930s, including *Rookery Nook* (1930), and *Thark* (1932). The latter – starring Lynn, Tom Walls, Robertson Hare and Mary Brough – was probably one of the best British comedies of the pre-war period, in terms of acting, directing and style, as well as being successful with the film-going public. One of its funniest scenes involved Lynn and Walls sharing a bedroom in a haunted house.

The trouble with British comedy, as with Robertson Hare, was that it knew its place and tried too hard not to offend. It was hardly surprising that the rising numbers of the working class who found the cinema a cheap and democratic place of entertainment should, on the whole, have preferred Chaplin and company.

Nevertheless, the public generally found the Aldwych farces on film amusing, as they did the films of Cicely Courtneidge and Jack Hulbert who, although obviously a middle-class product of public school, was a good chap, able to mix with the boys and full of the athletic vitality that the British admire. His good-humoured, long-chinned face was a happy addition to numerous comedies in the 1930s, in which he also danced more than

Cicely Courtneidge and Jack Hulbert step out in Under Your Hat *(British Lion, 1940).*

passably. He had a small part in the Elstree studio's musical revue, *Elstree Calling* (1930), then appeared with some success singing, dancing and being amusing in *Sunshine Susie* (*Office Girl* in US, 1931). Successful comedies he made with his actress wife, Cicely Courtneidge, included *Jack's the Boy* (1932), directed by Walter Forde, and *The Ghost Train* (1931).

Another comedian of the Thirties with a line of his own was Will Hay. Born in Stockton-on-Tees in 1888, Hay had spent most of his life on the music-hall stage. With Marcel Varnel as his director, he created a spendidly daft character – slightly lunatic, seedy in appearance, generally incompetent and, at times, something of a scoundrel. He was a schoolmaster in *Boys Will Be Boys* (1935), a prison governor in *Convict*

Ninety Nine (1937) and a railway station master in what was probably his best film, *Oh Mr Porter!* (1937), with his two frequent supporters – Graham Moffat as the rather dim fat boy and Moore Marriott as a dotty old man – in attendance. In the late Thirties, Hay joined Ealing Studios, where Basil Dearden co-directed him in his last comedies, including *The Black Sheep of Whitehall* (1941) in which he played the seedy head of a correspondence college with only one pupil, and *The Goose Steps Out* (1942), a nice piece of Nazi-lampooning.

While Ealing could hardly take the credit for introducing Hay to the British public, since he had joined them towards the end of his career, the studio was certainly the promoter of the film careers of Gracie Fields and George Formby, two of the most popular film entertainers in

Will Hay, Moore Marriott and Graham Moffat were well directed by Marcel Varnel to make Oh Mr Porter! *one of the best British comedies of the Thirties (Gainsborough, 1937).*

Gracie Fields coping with a cow down on the farm in Keep Smiling *(Rank, 1938).*

Britain in the Thirties and who were the main representatives of a significant change that was taking place in British society and in its entertainment: Fields and Formby were the working class come to break the hold of the middle classes on British films.

Gracie Fields was born in Rochdale in 1898 and was a stage singer and comedienne before Basil Dean put her into films. She was an instant success in 1931 with her first film, *Sally in Our Alley*,

directed by Maurice Elvey who had been working in British movies since 1913. Circumstances were propitious for the launch of Britain's first and most highly paid star comedienne: the Depression had just hit Britain, there were millions of unemployed, particularly in the north, and morale was low. 'Our Gracie' was hope personified; her Sally was a mill girl of indomitable spirit and unquenchable cheerfulness, just the recipe for the British working class who usually respond to challenges and the cruel blows of fate with good humour that is sometimes lacking when things are going well.

Gracie Fields was to be a top box-office draw for eight years, making such films as *Looking on the Bright Side* (1932), *This Week of Grace* (1933), and *Sing As We Go* (1934) written by J. B. Priestley. The last-named film, produced and directed by Basil Dean, was set and made on Blackpool's 'Golden Mile', the typical holiday resort of the British working class, where the enjoyment of life and romance was a strong contrast to the romantic holidays of virginal British ladies who went abroad to fall romantically in love with dark, handsome Austrians in *lederhosen*, as depicted in *Autumn Crocus*, which Basil Dean had also directed in the same year — clearly a man of catholic tastes and abilities!

By now, Gracie Fields was earning what for those times was the astronomical sum of £40,000 a picture and was being sought by Hollywood. She chose to stay in Britain to make films, one of which, *Queen of Hearts* (1936), was directed by the Italian-born Monty Banks, whom Gracie Fields married not long after. When the war came in 1939, rather than have him interned in Britain as an enemy alien, she accepted the Hollywood invitation and left her native shore, much to the indignation of her fans who saw her act as desertion. Her last films were made in America. Though her popularity waned over the years, Gracie Fields' contribution to the British cinema was rewarded when she was created Dame Commander of the Order of the British Empire in 1979, the year of her death; her reason for leaving Britain in 1939 had long since been understood and forgiven.

The loss of Gracie Fields created a crisis at Ealing, for she was one of their biggest attractions at the box-office. The problem was soon resolved by the promotion of George Formby, who was already on the

Lobbycard for Shipyard Sally, 'Our Gracie's' last made-in-Britain movie. After it, Gracie Fields moved to Hollywood (Twentieth Century Productions, 1939).

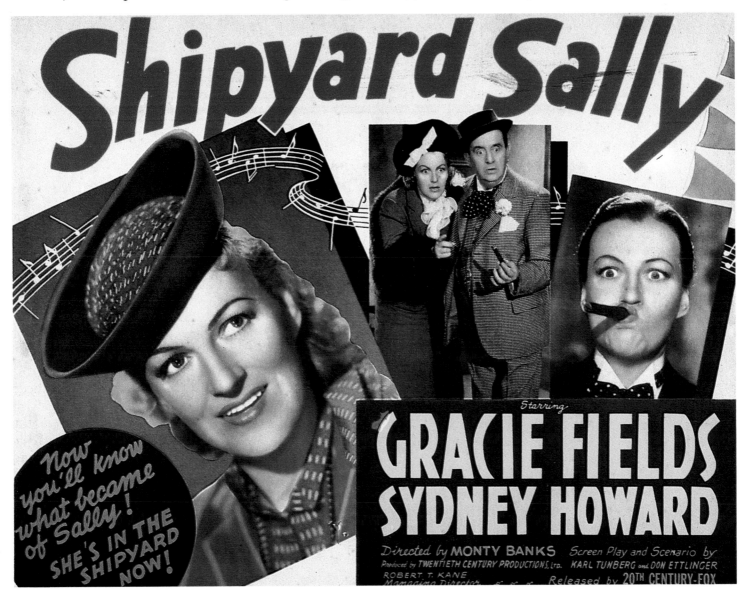

Ealing payroll. In a sense he was a male version of the Fields' personality, since he was also of northern working-class stock. He was born in Wigan in 1904, and was a Lancashire lad with a ukelele and cheeky grin, which endeared him to a wide public. Formby was a simple man with simple tastes, of which one was high-speed motorbikes, so for one of his early Ealing films, *No Limit* (1935), Basil Dean engaged Walter Greenwood, author of the realistic play about the north, *Love on the Dole*, to write a story about a young man who dreams of taking part in the Isle of Man TT race.

Formby's films were made for the market created by Gracie Fields, though they tended to be much simpler-minded and contained more slapstick, and did not add much that was new to British cinema comedy except for his songs, which had a naughty seaside-postcard type of humour that opened the door to future jokes about subjects that had formerly been discreetly ignored. Unlike Gracie Fields' films, Formby's were seldom exported to America, as his low, working-class humour just did not travel.

Basil Dean was an extremely active and dynamic man who not only introduced Gracie Fields and George Formby to films but also had a hand in many other serious and ambitious dramas. However, he did not achieve much financial success in his operations at Ealing and eventually there came a disagreement with his backers, which led to his resignation. He was replaced by Michael Balcon who had had considerable and wide experience of the film industry through his connection with Gainsborough Pictures and Gaumont British at Lime Grove.

Building on the foundations laid by Basil Dean, Balcon set out to turn round Ealing's fortunes. He engaged Walter Forde to make comedies for the studio, one of which, called *Cheer Boys Cheer* (1939), could be seen as the prototype for the famous Ealing comedies. The film dealt with the rivalry between two brewers, one representing cosy-old-pub British way of drinking and the other a brash new, chromium-plated style that portended the future. The film, with its various plots and confrontations between the two brewers, aided and abetted by Graham Moffatt and Moore Marriott, was a romp that explored the humorous

possibilities of a well-loved British way of life. In this, it was a forerunner of the kind of British movie comedies with which the names of Ealing and Michael Balcon are indissolubly connected.

Cheer Boys Cheer appeared in British cinemas on the eve of World War II, and while it was the last of this kind of film that British studios would produce until the end of the war, this does not mean that comedies were not made in Britain during these years. Film-making now had to support the war effort, and many films, both serious and comic, were produced to press home important messages and to boost morale. One of the first wartime comedies was *Sailors Three* (*Three Cock-eyed Sailors* in US, 1940), Forde's last film at Ealing, with Tommy Trinder, Claude Hulbert and Michael Wilding starring. The plot concerned British sailors getting drunk while on shore leave in an American port and returning by mistake to the German pocket battleship *Ludendorff* instead of their own ship. George Formby, too, was quickly in morale-boosting form in *Let George Do It* (1940) in which, as a member of a concert party bound for Blackpool, he ends up in Norway as an unwitting intelligence man.

Formby's film was directed by Marcel Varnel, who was also responsible for Will Hay's successful contribution to the war effort, the aforementioned *The Goose Steps Out* (1942). This was a fine vehicle for Hays' inept and scoundrel-like muddler whom British intelligence forces to take the place of his Nazi spy double. Hays returns to Germany in the spy's guise where he finds that the Nazis are just as big bunglers as he is, but he is luckier and therefore manages to outwit them.

An unusual comedy film to appear in wartime was *The Life and Death of Colonel Blimp* (1943), produced and directed by Michael Powell for his and Emeric Pressburger's new company, Archer Films. The character of Blimp – or Colonel Clive Wynn-Candy VC, to give him his full designation – was a creation of Low, the political cartoonist, who made the Colonel represent all the old-fashioned ways, not only of the British army but of the whole British establishment. The problem of producing a film that criticized the army leaders in the midst of war was overcome by a statement shown in the opening credits. This

film is dedicated to the New Army of Britain, to the new spirit in warfare, to the new toughness in battle and to the men and women who know what they are fighting for and are fighting this war to win it.' It sounded as if it had been written by a public relations expert.

Blimp, played by Roger Livesey, plays out his military life from the Boer war to the Blitz of the Second World War, during which he develops a friendship for a German, played by Anton Walbrook. The young Deborah Kerr took three different roles – all women from various stages in Blimp's life. The film was one of the few major wartime films to be shot in Technicolor, which was generally little used because of the difficulty of getting film stock and equipment.

As the fortunes of war changed and the need to make propagandist films diminished, the studios began once more to supply what the public wanted, which in the final year of the war were escapist films of the type being produced by Hollywood. At first, this was doled out in the same style of comedy slapstick and farce as in films before the war, and even the

Anton Walbrook, Deborah Kerr and Roger Livesey in The Life and Death of Colonel Blimp *(GFD/ Archers, 1943).*

actors who played in them were the same as in pre-war years; Tommy Trinder and Sonnie Hale appeared in *Fiddlers Three* (1944), a fantasy comedy about two soldiers on leave who get transported back in time to ancient Rome; Flanagan and Allen of the Crazy Gang made a sentimental comedy, *Dreaming* (1945); and both films came from Ealing. However most escapism in the latter part of the war was in the form of thrillers or films that evoked Britain's past achievements, whether in war as *Henry V* (1944), or in literature, such as *Great Expectations* made by David Lean in 1946, or dwelt sentimentally on British rural life like *The Loves of Joanna Godden* (1947). It seemed, in fact, as if, after the traumatic experience of the war, Britain was trying to rediscover her identity.

There was also another force at work. The working class, which had found pre-war expression in the films of Gracie Fields and George Formby, was now changing social and political life in Britain and, in 1945, had for the first time voted in a socialist government, albeit one heavily larded with middle-class graduates of Oxbridge. This government under Clement Attlee carried out a far-reaching programme of reforms, including nationalization and the establishment of a state, which promised a new and better life for all, raising hopes and expectations throughout the country. Those who had given Labour a landslide victory were also the backbone of the cinema-going public, which averaged 30 million people a year in the years leading up to the apogee of the new Utopia, the Festival of Britain of 1951.

It seems ironic that this euphoric period of working-class liberation and expectation should have been marked by comedy films that were very often concerned with distinctly middle-class whimsies and attitudes. The Ealing comedies are among the most successful series of films ever made in Britain and are real gems of British film comedy, although perhaps their overseas success had something to do with the American love of such English traditions as Morris dancing and afternoon teas in thatched cottages.

The Ealing comedies reflect in their kindly and humorous, but often also sharply satiric, way all that is worst and best in the English character: its lunatic fringe and its rational core, its chauvinism and its tolerance, its pomposity and its

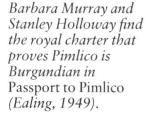

Barbara Murray and Stanley Holloway find the royal charter that proves Pimlico is Burgundian in Passport to Pimlico *(Ealing, 1949).*

self-depreciation and, above all, its ability to deflate the pretensions of others. These films also display a sophistication of attitude to morality, society and the world in general hardly seen before in British film comedy.

The year 1949 was Ealing's *annus mirabilis*, in which three immortal comedies – *Passport to Pimlico*, *Whisky Galore!* and *Kind Hearts and Coronets* – appeared. In *Passport to Pimlico*, the finding of treasure trove during a search for an unexploded bomb in London results in the discovery of a document showing that this corner of London was granted to the Duke of Burgundy in perpetuity back in the Middle Ages. Thus the inhabitants of Pimlico suddenly find that, far from being British, they are Burgundians and therefore not subject to the post-war aggravations of food rationing, exchange limitations and other annoying regulations. Instantly, the bank manager takes control of the bank's funds in the name of Burgundy, the local pub abandons licensing hours and all the shops sell everything they can lay their hands on, while the inhabitants give way to the heady excitements of their new-found freedom. A waterside pleasure beach, pavement cafés and other Continental delights spring up in the narrow, bomb-damaged streets.

Unfortunately, Burgundian Pimlico is a landlocked enclave and the British government closes its frontiers, placing under seige the new dukedom in London's midst. The inhabitants are incensed and, in one of the film's most memorable lines, declare that they have always been English, and it's because they're English that they are sticking to their right to be Burgundians. In the end, Pimlico opts to return to Britain and the British government respond magnanimously by organizing a reunion party at which new ration books and identity cards are issued.

The director of this wonderful romp, where the ever-increasing lunacy is set against realistic and familiar streets and buildings, was Henry Cornelius, and the cast list is a roll-call of the great and good in British acting, including Margaret Rutherford, Hermione Baddeley, Stanley Holloway (as the grocer), Raymond Huntley (the bank manager) Charles Hawtrey and numerous others.

Whisky Galore! (*Tight Little Island* in US) also dealt with independence.

Captain Waggett (Basil Radford) thinks he's found some of the illicit whisky hidden all over little Todday, but it is the pub's legal quota. A nice moment from Whisky Galore! *(Ealing/Michael Balcon Production, 1949).*

The story this time was by Compton Mackenzie, who based his tale on a real incident when a ship carrying whisky to the United States was wrecked off the small island of Eriskay in the Outer Hebrides. The inhabitants of *Whisky Galore*'s Todday, like those of Eriskay, decided that its cargo could justifiably be considered as lawful salvage, and a great deal of the precious 'water of life' found its way into hands far from the Customs and Excise department.

In the film, Captain Waggett (Basil Radford), captain of the local Home Guard, tries to prevent the natives from getting hold of the whisky, while the islanders headed by Dr Maclaren

Kind Hearts and Coronets, directed by Robert Hamer, carried the idea of personal freedom a big step further. Louis Mazzini (Dennis Price) decides that his right to the title of the aristocratic d'Ascoyne family entitles him to knock off everyone in the line of succession between him and the dukedom. Here, the comedy is black indeed, and the style cool, elegantly ironic, especially as played by Dennis Price who was an urbane and very civilized murderer throughout. When one of the d'Ascoynes was drowned with his girlfriend on the Thames at Maidenhead – Mazzini's efforts, of course – Mazzini, while apologetic about the girl's demise, reflects that she had, after all, already suffered the fate worse than death the night before.

The film was also something of a *tour de force* by Alec Guinness, who played no fewer than eight members (male and female) of the unfortunate family who stood between Mazzini and his goal. Guinness also played a leading role in the highly successful *Lavender Hill Mob* (1951), in which he and Stanley Holloway devised a brilliant scheme for smuggling gold. The latter was to be stolen by Bank of England employee Guinness, and secreted into France as models of the Eiffel Tower.

The Ealing comedies achieved a standard of film comedy never reached before in Britain. Although some were better than others, all were entertaining and gave ample scope for the talents of many newcomers who would be among Britain's finest comic actors. There was Peter Sellers, for instance, who appeared as a teddy boy crook in *The Ladykillers* (1955), the last of the comedies. Superbly directed by Alexander Mackendrick, *The Ladykillers* dealt with a bunch of criminals headed by Professor Marcus (Alec Guinness) who rented a room from Mrs. Wilberforce (Katie Johnson) ostensibly as a practice room for a chamber orchestra, the members of which included, as well as Sellers, Cecil Parker as a bogus major, Herbert Lom as a hit man and Danny Green as a dim strong man called 'One Round'. The room was really rented as a centre of operations for a bank robbery; however the sweet little old lady found out, so they had to kill her but could not decide which of them was to do the deed. As the film developed, the criminals killed

Above: Kind Hearts and Coronets *was Ealing comedy at its best – gentle, charming, urbane and very funny (Ealing, 1949).*

Opposite: Alec Guinness and Stanley Holloway elated at the successful outcome of their plan to relieve the Bank of England of a million pounds-worth of gold bullion; a poster for The Lavender Hill Mob *(Ealing, 1951).*

(James Robertson Justice) are determined that they will have it. The fun is fast and furious and though the story might at first seem to be just a hilarious fantasy, it can also be seen to represent changes in society, where the old standards of law and order are breaking down and people are beginning to put personal freedom of action and decision above the requirements of the law.

Whisky Galore! was directed by Alexander Mackendrick who, born in the United States, made many very fine films for Ealing. He directed *Whisky Galore!* in a realistic style very close to that of the great British documentary film-makers of the 1930s and 1940s, which helped lift the film from the realm of the merely prettily comic to the very best human comedy.

The last of the great Ealing comedies, The Ladykillers, *allowed innocent old lady Katie Johnson to keep the loot stolen by a gang led by Alec Guinness. The gang (background, left to right) were Peter Sellers, Danny Green, Cecil Parker and Herbert Lom (Ealing/ Michael Balcon Productions, 1955).*

each other off, the last one being done in by the dropping arm of a signal as he threw his victim over a railway bridge. The little old lady was left with the loot from the robbery.

Although many of the Ealing comedies were simply amusing frolics with only a slight underlying message, one at least, *The Man in the White Suit* (1951) also directed by Mackendrick, was concerned with social comment – in this instance, a protest against the methods of industry and the connivance of employers and unions when it suited both sides. Its star was Alec Guinness as the young man who discovers a formula for a fibre that will not wear out. This disconcerts both the capitalists and the workers for, if released to the public, it would mean that the mill where the young man works would be closed down and all the workers would be redundant. Fortunately, the situation is

resolved by a flaw in the formula that makes the suit fall apart just as its inventor, Sidney Stratton, is about to be set upon by both sides.

It might have been thought that *The Man in the White Suit* would presage a more near-the-bone style of satirical comedy about the problems of society, like that which was developing in France and Italy around this time, but it was not until the Sixties had nearly arrived that the battle between capital and labour, employers and unions, hit the screen in another superb satirical comedy.

The Boulting brothers' production of *I'm All Right, Jack* (1959) with Peter Sellers in the lead as the bone-headed shop steward, Fred Kite, reflected much of the trouble that had been brewing in British society since the end of the war. The problem facing Britain was simply that the expectations aroused by successive

112

post-war governments had not really been fulfilled, partly because, as standards of living improved, so expectations rose further, and partly because foreign competition was undercutting old British markets throughout the world; the result was disenchantment and suspicion. *I'm All Right, Jack* told the story of Stanley Windrush (Ian Carmichael) who is a rather incompetent middle-class university product aspiring to a management job for which he is clearly not suited. He starts off on the shop floor, but is soon in trouble for working too hard and runs foul of Kite, thus causing a strike that upsets both management and union, who together connive to get rid of him. Windrush decides to retire from the fray altogether, just as his father had done, and so opts out like others of his class, joining his father at a nudist camp where the old boy is enjoying his retirement.

Among the array of acting talent in the film, Irene Handl stands out as Kite's wife, Richard Attenborough and Dennis Price as two examples of the smooth, double-dyed boardroom class, and John Le Mesurier as a twitching time-and-motion study man.

By this time, Peter Sellers' career was really taking off and he had won a large following among the more intellectually aware of Britain's cinema-going audiences, initially attracted by his part in the wonderfully surrealistic BBC radio series, *The Goon Show*. He had the lead role in the highly successful film version of Kingsley Amis's novel *That Uncertain Feeling*, called *Only Two Can Play* (1962) and directed and co-produced by Sidney Gilliat from a script by Brian Forbes. Sellers played a librarian in a Welsh town who gets involved with a wealthy local dignitary's sexy blonde wife, played by

Personnel man Terry Thomas under attack from union leader Peter Sellers and a cohort of brother workers in I'm All Right, Jack, *John Boulting's satiric look at British labour relations (British Lion, 1959).*

Mai Zetterling. Richard Attenborough appeared as a boring pseudo-intellectual – a favourite Kingsley Amis type, as seen in his first novel *Lucky Jim*, the 1957 film version of which had been turned by the Boulting Brothers into a feeble romp, far from Amis's original satire.

As the Fifties wore on, the great films from Ealing, and such near-look-alikes as the amusing though more coarsely slap-stick *Genevieve* (1953), about the veteran car race to Brighton, began to look like works from a lost era of glory. On the whole, the British comedy production-line was turning out the same innocuous, non-intellectual mixture as in the bad days of the 1930s, much comedy reduced to end-less gags and grimaces and trousers falling down or being torn off, or Norman Wis-dom's imitation of Chaplin combined with large overdoses of maudlin pathos. The low point seemed to be reached by the shambolic and risible 'Carry On' ser-ies, which began in 1958 with *Carry On, Sergeant*.

This was, however, what the new society seemed to want and these films were not only successes but went on into long series. The subtle and low-keyed approach of the Ealing comedies was replaced by broad comedy that, even at its highest level – as in the entertaining *Doctor in the House* series, based on the books by Richard Gordon and starring actors such as Dirk Bogarde, James Robertson Justice and Donald Sinden – hardly reached the artistic levels being achieved at the same time by Continental and American film-makers.

During this period, there was an effort to create an international exchange in the art of the cinema, with American writers and directors making films in England and, more occasionally, visits by masters of European cinema, especially the French, but the effect on comedy film production and style in Britain was slight. It seemed for a time as if the film business were descending into a slough of banality dictated by popular taste. Fortunately,

Kay Kendall, Kenneth More and canine friend have trouble with their ancient motor in Genevieve, *a delightfully funny tale set against the background of the annual London-Brighton veteran car run (Rank/Sirius Productions, 1953).*

this was not so, and the forces that had been evolving through films from *Sally in Our Alley* right through to *I'm All Right, Jack* were ready to break out with renewed vigour.

They showed up with considerable impact in two startlingly different British-produced comedies, *Dr Strangelove, or How I Learned to Stop Worrying and Love the Bomb* (1964) and *Tom Jones* (1963).

Dr Strangelove, produced, directed and partly written by Stanley Kubrick, was a very black comedy indeed, in which an American B52 bomber flies towards the USSR carrying a live nuclear bomb, ordered there by a manic general, Jack D. Ripper (Sterling Hayden), who then seals Burpelson Air Force Base off from the outside world so that the order cannot be countermanded. Peter Sellers had three roles in the film: Dr Strangelove, the ex-Nazi scientist and creator of the bomb, whose wooden arm keeps trying to make the Nazi salute; Merkin J. Muffley, President of the United States; and an RAF officer, Group Captain Lionel Mandrake.

The mercilessly mocking comedy of *Dr Strangelove* was given a nail-biting suspense, not often encountered in comedy film, by director Stanley Kubrick's brilliant and ever-faster cutting between scenes on the ground in the Pentagon ('Gentlemen, you can't fight in here – this is the War Room,' liberal President Muffley is moved to cry during the debate on how to stop the bomber) or at the Air Force Base, and in the air, where the B52, flown by Major 'King' Kong (Slim Pickens), is getting ever nearer its target. The film ends with Major Kong riding his bomb earthwards to the accompaniment of Vera Lynn singing 'We'll Meet Again'.

Beneath the grim laughter, *Dr Strangelove* was a coldly intellectual film, surrealistic and finely controlled. *Tom Jones* was the opposite in every department, a wonderfully warm, sexually bawdy and colourful film full of life and laughter, though it was not without a satirical bite as well. Director Tony Richardson reached right back to the Mack Sennett two-reeler for many of his film devices – speeded-up action, sub-titles superimposed on the picture, frozen frame and many more – all to tell Henry Fielding's classic 18th-century story. The stars were all straight actors with British theatre training – Albert Finney (Tom), Susannah York, Hugh Griffith and Dame Edith Evans among others – and Richardson kept the whole thing going with such style, including one of the most erotic eating sequences ever seen in the movies,

Above: Lecherous Alfie (Michael Caine) tries his charm on rich American Shelley Winters in Alfie, *the film that shot Caine to international stardom (Paramount/Sheldrake, 1966).*

Opposite: Albert Finney and Diane Cilento getting closely acquainted in Tom Jones *(United Artists/Woodfall, 1963).*

that it was no wonder that *Tom Jones* won four Oscars: Best Picture, Best Director, Best Screenplay and Best Film Score.

A variety of modern Tom Jones was the hero of Lewis Gilbert's *Alfie* (1966), also a Sixties' landmark film of a kind, since it launched Michael Caine into the superstar bracket, the count-down to which he had begun the year before with *The Ipcress File*. Unlike Albert Finney's Arthur Seaton in *Saturday Night and Sunday Morning* (1960), who was a rather brutish working-class lad in the English 'kitchen sink' drama tradition, Alfie was the new, smooth type, trying to cross the line into the middle-class world. He walked the London scene in a blue blazer with an unidentifiable but impressive badge on the breast pocket, and he knew how to talk softly to the birds to charm them off their perches. However, the birds demonstrated that they, too, were moving on in the new society, and Alfie was left dangling.

On the whole, the Sixties in British comedy films was the decade of the workers who had made it or were making it to the top in business, fashion, finance and the arts, a society more concerned with making it than with worrying about the workers. For example, in *Nothing but the Best* (1963), directed by Clive Donner, in which Alan Bates played the lead, one of screenwriter Frederic Raphael's best scenes has the seedy product of an English public school (Denholm Elliott) teaching the working-class hero how to make the boss's daughter.

One of the group of working-class lads who had made it in dazzling style was The Beatles, whose first film was the enjoyable *A Hard Day's Night* (1964), in which the plot was minimal, the gags fun and the Beatles songs among their best. The film was directed by Richard Lester, the American-born movie-maker who had introduced a spirit of sheer lunacy into the

Rita Tushingham looks worried about where she's heading in The Knack *(United Artists/Woodfall Films, 1965).*

Sixties with his directing of *The Running, Jumping and Standing Still Film* (1960), a brilliant screen crystallization of the very popular radio series, *The Goon Show*. The film was exactly what its title said, with the radio show's stars Spike Milligan, Peter Sellers and Harry Secombe doing the running, jumping and standing still. Lester was also in charge of *The Knack* (in the US, *The Knack . . . and How to Get It*, 1965), in which Rita Tushingham, Michael Crawford and Ray Brooks coped with one of the most popular subjects of the Sixties: sex. Ray Brooks was the one with the knack, Michael Crawford wished he had it and Rita Tushingham was the one on whom both men experimented with using it. Like the second Beatles' film, *Help!*, which Lester also directed in 1965, *The Knack* was fresh and exuberant at the time, but has not worn well with the passage of years.

Rather better, perhaps because its cast was so good, was *Georgy Girl* (1966), which latched on to the theme of *The Knack*, though from the girl's point of view. Lynn Redgrave was very good indeed as Georgy, the plain but warm and lovable girl who was not a success with men, and Charlotte Rampling was her flat mate who was. The men in their lives were Alan Bates and – surprise! – James Mason.

Lynn Redgrave teamed up with Rita Tushingham for *Smashing Time* (1967) a comedy about two girls trying to make it in London where everything was supposed to be swinging. But even when the film appeared, the lively optimism of the Sixties was beginning to subside, the Beatles had become an institution, and the brave new world was looking more and more like *Animal Farm* played in a James Bond setting.

James Mason clearly thinks that Lynn Redgrave is going over the top in her baby department purchases: a scene from Georgy Girl *(Columbia/Everglades, 1966).*

119

Opposite:
Appearances to the
contrary, Dirk
Bogarde and Monica
Vitti were on opposing
sides in the
extravagant goings-on
in Modesty Blaise
(Twentieth Century-
Fox, 1966).

Below: Sid James
enjoying the view in
Carry On Dick, the
26th Carry On film.
Providing the scenery
is Barbara Windsor,
another long-serving
member of the Carry
On team (Rank/Peter
Rogers Production,
1974).

Joseph Losey, the American director who had begun working in Britain at the time of the McCarthy witch hunts, parodied the James Bond style and the Sixties themselves in *Modesty Blaise* (1966), an extravaganza based on the comic strip. With its gimmicky op-art backgrounds and stylized camp acting by Monica Vitti as the eponymous heroine, Terence Stamp as her sidekick William Garvin, and Dirk Bogarde as the white-coiffeured villain Gabriel, the film was a send-up of itself as much as of its period.

By the time the 1970s got under way, the surface self-assurance of the 'Swinging Sixties' had begun to give at the seams, not least in the British film industry. Cinema attendances were falling off, cinemas were closing at a greater rate than ever and backers with money were difficult to find. In the circumstances, it is not surprising that makers of comedy films aimed at the lowest common denominator more and more often, trying to trawl the biggest audiences with films like the 'Carry on' series, which by 1973 numbered twenty-five features. At their best, these were examples of grassroot comedy of the simplest kind, with familiar and predictable jokes and comic situations. At the least, they gave regular employment to a practised team, which generally included Sid James, Kenneth Williams, Kenneth Connor, Jim Dale, Hattie Jacques, Joan Sims, Bernard Breslaw, Barbara Windsor and Terry Scott.

Television was also rifled for cinema fodder, from such basic sit-coms as *On the Buses*, which provided a mini-series of three movies, starting with a film of the same title in 1971, to the more way-out *Monty Python's Flying Circus*, which gave rise to a series of Python films starting with *And Now for Something Completely Different* in 1971 and going on to such up-lifting subjects as *Monty*

Python and the Holy Grail (1975), ... *The Life of Brian* (1979), and ... *The Meaning of Life* (1983).

The Monty Python team has split up in recent years to go solo. In the case of the 'special effects' expert and film director, Terry Gilliam, this has meant excursions into a fantasy world where the humour has become increasingly cruel, from *Jabberwocky* (1977) and *Time Bandits* (1981) to *Brazil* (1985), an extraordinary parody of the world of *1984*. Michael Palin, on the other hand, has now been acting in a more straightforward style in the enjoyable comedy of Edwardian sexual manners, *The Missionary* (1983), and in the great success of 1985, the much-praised *A Private Function*, based on a story by Alan Bennett, who also wrote the screenplay.

A Private Function took a rude and farcical look at post-war snobbery in Yorkshire, when ration books and all the rest of the depressing paraphernalia of the late Forties were all too important in everyone's lives. Michael Palin was a socially unacceptable chiropodist who kidnaps a pig. Maggie Smith, who had also starred with Palin in *The Missionary*, was the wife, desperate for respectability, who had to pursue the incontinent animal around her house with a butcher's knife.

On the whole, the 1980s have seen a

Above: A regal role for veteran British comedian Max Wall, playing King Bruno the Questionable in Terry Gilliam's Jabberwocky *(Columbia/Umbrella Films, 1977).*

Opposite: Getting across the message of Christmas in Monty Python's The Meaning of Life *(HandMade Films, 1983).*

123

definite up-swing in the quality of movie comedy being produced in Britain. Some of it has come from the British stage, including *The National Health* (1983) – based on Peter Nichols' satirical look at the way the British national health service functions ... or doesn't – and *Educating Rita* (1984), based on Willy Russell's stage play about the relationship between a college lecturer and the girl in search of an intellectual education as a way of improving her lot in life.

The National Health Service was, on the face of it, taking a battering again in Lindsay Anderson's blood-stained and anarchic farce, *Britannia Hospital* (1982) – journalist Malcolm McDowell, investigating the truth behind the strikes at the hospital, gets his head transplanted for his pains – but it was soon apparent that it was the state of Britain as a whole that Anderson had in mind, not just the health service, and it was a terminal case he was depicting.

After which, it is no little relief to look at the work of a director who has been the

Maggie Smith and Michael Palin in pursuit of an incontinent pig called Betty in A Private Function *(HandMade Films, 1984).*

brightest spot in British comic movie production in the 1980s. Bill Forsyth, a determinedly Scottish film-maker from Glasgow, caught the film world's attention with *That Sinking Feeling* in 1979. This was a jaunty comedy-thriller about unemployed young people from Glasgow's slums, told with a sharp eye for background and a fine ear for the nuances of Scottish life. Then came the very delightful *Gregory's Girl* (1980), set in Scotland's Cumbernauld New Town. Gregory was an attractive if somewhat callow youth, played by Gordon John Sinclair, who lost his heart, and his place in the school soccer team, to the delicious Dorothy (Dee Hepburn). The tracing of Gregory's trek through the bewildering labyrinth of teenage love to some sort of conclusion on a balmy summer's night was directed by Forsyth with a warm, yet sharp, humour.

By the time of his third film, *Local Hero* (1983), also set in Scotland, Forsyth had entered the league of the big budget movie, complete with 'Big Star', Burt Lancaster. The film, seen by its maker as 'a cross between *Brigadoon* and *Apocalypse Now*', concerned the crisis that came to a quiet, remote, Scottish sea-coast village when an American oil company chose it

as the site for their latest development scheme. The villagers, oblivious to the disastrous effect the plan would have on the local ecology, were all for it and the money it would bring; the local beachcomber, something of an amateur astrologer, was against it. Fortunately for him and, eventually, for the village, too, the oil tycoon (Lancaster) was a star-gazer.

A year later, Forsyth came out with *Comfort and Joy*, about a war among Glasgow's ice-cream van men, and a parody of all those Hollywood gangster movies of years gone by. It was also a story of a man's search, largely unsuccessful, for his own inner self, with disc jockey Bill Paterson trying to come to terms with his life, what he has done with it so far, and what he hopes for it in the future. The tone was still comic, but there were suggestions that Forsyth was also looking for something else in his work. It will be one of the more interesting studies of the 1980s to see just how Bill Forsyth's career develops.

On the whole, the future for the British comic movie looks promising, and the rich fund of talent in directors, writers and actors that Britain possesses surely portends good things.

Dorothy, Gregory's Girl, has replaced Gregory in the school's football team, but he's too much in love to mind; Dee Hepburn and Gordon John Sinclair in goal. (Samuel Goldwyn/ Lake Film Productions, 1980).

THAT UNCERTAIN FEELING:
THE MOVIE COMEDY IN EUROPE

Here, we are considering European comic movies that made an impression on world cinema, rather than the many that were made for home consumption and not intended to cross international boundaries. These boundaries had been easier to cross in the early days of silent movies, when film-makers everywhere were learning the business and borrowing from such traditional forms of entertainment as the circus, vaudeville, the music hall and theatre. A clown was a clown was a clown, and since he was probably also a mime artist, his work could be shown to audiences in many countries without difficulty.

Count Malcolm (Jarl Kuele) and Countess Charlotte (Margit Carlquist) in dramatic mood in Ingmar Bergman's Smiles of a Summer Night *(Rank/ Svensk Filmindustri, 1955).*

When the clown had to speak, however, his audiences shrank dramatically, and a different kind of comedy had to be created to win back world audiences. The Mexican-born Cantinflas, for instance, had to act in an American film before the non-Spanish-speaking world noticed him. A tent-show buffoon, circus clown and acrobat, he developed from the mid-1930s into one of the most popular film comics in the, admittedly large, Spanish-speaking world, but few outside that had heard of him until Mike Todd cast him as Passepartout in *Around the World in Eighty Days* (1956). His popularity was great – and short-lived. After the commercial failure of *Pépé*, made in 1960, he went back to Spanish-speaking films and has been little heard of since.

Ingmar Bergman claimed a place for Sweden in world film comedy with his wonderfully warm comedy of sex and manners, *Sommarnattens Leende* (*Smiles of a Summer Night*, 1955). The Greeks who, after all, wrote the world's earliest comic plays, which reached great heights of sophistication and political audacity in the works of Aristophanes (some of which have been filmed), have occasionally produced modern comedies that have made film buffs, at least, sit up and take notice; and so have film-makers in the Soviet Union. A recent film from a Soviet director was the made-in-France *Les Favoris de la Lune* (*Favourites of the Moon*, 1985), in which the Georgian director Otar Yosseliani painted a sparkling comic picture of Parisian life. But, of all the countries in Europe, Italy and France have proved the most successful at finding the way to make movie comedy with international appeal, and their work provides most of the films discussed in this chapter.

Soviet film-maker
Otar Iosseliani looked
at the lives of a cross-
section of Parisians in
his Favourites of the
Moon (International
Spectrafilm, 1985).

In Europe, the idea of making comedy films that would knock traditional social values and mores, and perhaps change them through laughter, grew up rather later than in America. Perhaps it was because the established and basically accepted social order, give or take a war or a revolution or two, and the respect in which such institutions as church, government and law were generally held inhibited Europeans from putting their fingers to their noses and waggling them. While much early European film comedy seemed to grow naturally out of the old *commedia dell'arte* and clown tradition – and these films after all, were not so unlike early American ones, with their reliance on men and women with vaudeville training – they remained on the level of the banana-skin farce or of the trivial domestic situation for longer than in the United States. Even the great Max Linder,

said to have been one of the formative influences on Charlie Chaplin, did not develop much beyond this kind of film.

While there were exceptions, of course – and Ernst Lubitsch, working in Berlin, where he had been a successful 'character' comedian in films before and during the First World War, must be considered one of the greatest – it seemed as if these exceptions were permissible only if it were not home and hearth that were being lampooned. It was all right, for instance, to mock the manners and customs of foreigners, as Lubitsch did in 1919 in one of his early directorial triumphs, *Die Austern Prinzessin* (*The Oyster Princess*), in which he took a wry, satirical look at Americans and their way of life.

By the 1920s, European film-makers were on the whole still devoting most of their big efforts to the production of grand epics glorifying tradition and history or to fantasies and such spine-chillers as Robert Wiene's *Das Kabinett des Dr. Caligari* (*The Cabinet of Dr. Caligari*, 1919) and F. W. Murnau's *Nosferatu, Eine Symphonie des Gravens* (*Nosferatu, a Symphony of Terrors*, 1922). Lubitsch himself made as many grand historical dramas as comedies in Germany before going on to his enormously successful career in America.

The notion of making comments upon society via full-length comedy features came to Europe from America, particularly through the films of Charlie Chaplin and the great American comics; their influence on European and other comedy film-makers around the world was immeasurable. Go to the cinema in Britain or Italy, Chile or Argentina, Australia or Spain in the 1920s and you were much more likely to be watching Chaplin, Keaton or Arbuckle than any home-grown comic.

In France, two writer–directors, René Clair and Jean Renoir, who began making films from the mid-Twenties and whose impact and influence were universal, were themselves influenced in some degree by Chaplin, though they both went on to develop highly individual and personal styles during the course of their long working lives.

René Clair was born René-Lucien Chomette in 1898 in Paris, where his father kept a shop in the market quarter of Les Halles. He began taking an interest in the theatre as a child, but by the time he had left his teens behind, that interest had turned to films.

Clair was a man of his time, torn between nostalgia for the stable life of pre-First World War Europe, and the dissatisfaction that he felt for the world in which he now found himself, dissatisfaction that was being loudly and widely expressed by the left-wing intellectuals of Paris among whom Clair lived. He came to blame the imperfections of society on the life of urban and industrial capitalism that promised material well-being but sapped the innate natural goodness of humanity. In cities and factories, Clair believed, people were forced to seek false values to compensate for their unnatural mode of life, becoming greedy for power and money, the pursuit of which led to a social system that would bring them neither happiness nor satisfaction.

These ideas, to be seen in Chaplin's comedies of this period, were characteristic of Clair's films almost from the beginning. Thus, in the early film *Paris qui dort* (*The Crazy Ray*, 1924), many of the world's inhabitants have been paralyzed by a deadly ray and the rest, freed from the moral pressures of society and in fear of their lives, indulge in orgies of looting desirable objects that no longer have value now that the society that prized them has

Ernest Lubitsch on the set of Das Weib des Pharao *(Wives of the Pharaoh), 1921, with Emil Jannings resplendent in Ancient Egyptian costume.*

Right: True friendship between men was a theme in René Clair's A Nous la Liberté, *in which he commented wryly on the modern industrial world in which people become machines (Tobis, 1931).*

Below: When it looks as if the wedding to which they have been invited might not take place, the guests try to take back their presents: a scene from René Clair's comedy of manners, An Italian Straw Hat *(Albatross, 1927).*

foundered. A comedy! Well, yes, because Clair is laughing at the stupidity of these people and telling his mad joke with a light, dancing touch.

In 1927, Clair made *Un Chapeau de Paille d'Italie* (An Italian Straw Hat), one of the masterpieces of silent film comedy. It was his sixth film as writer and director, and was a comedy of manners in which society was made fun of via its rituals and possessions. In this story of true love overcoming all obstacles to marriage, Clair makes the cynical point that marriage has become a ritual of acquisition whose true meaning has been obscured by social pretension and ambition, allowing his camera to concentrate on the social props to the wedding – the overdressed guests, the ostentatious décor of the room, the pretentious gifts which, when it seems for a moment that the wedding might not take place, are nearly snatched back – rather than on the marriage itself.

The brotherhood of man as the central moral force of life was celebrated by Clair in two great films, *Sous les Toits de Paris* (*Under the Roofs of Paris*, 1930) and *A Nous la Liberté* (*To Us Liberty*, 1931). *Sous les Toits de Paris*, Clair's first sound picture, was the story of two comrades who share the same girlfriend, a theme that appeared again thirty years later in another French film, Françoise Truffaut's *Jules et Jim*, though in this later work, the protagonists' playing at life as if it were a game ended in tragedy. René Clair's solution to his protagonists' problem was to have them throw dice – a rather ungallant way to settle things, taking no account of the girl's wishes, but Clair was always more concerned with the idea than the reality of his tale, a platonic approach characteristic of his work. *A Nous la Liberté* is also about two men, Albert and Louis, who are from different levels of society but have shared the common experience of being in jail together, and have developed the bond of loyalty and comradeship that, Clair suggests, is open to all people.

Clair was a master at creating a total integration of plot and visual image in his films. In *Le Million* (1931), a story about two men in pursuit of a lottery ticket, Clair created ballet-like sequences of crowds rushing about, Keystone-style policemen chasing each other aimlessly across the screen, a hilarious game in a

theatre. Absurdity was piled on absurdity with an unmatchable lightness of touch.

Clair was at his best working in France in a French atmosphere, and the films of his English and American periods, during the Second World War, though never less than entertaining, sometimes showed a preoccupation with fantasy that went over the top. However, *The Ghost Goes West*, made in England in 1935, was great fun, as was one of his American films, *I Married a Witch* (1942). Back in France after the war, one of his most memorable films was *La Beauté du Diable* (Beauty and the Devil, 1950) starring the handsome, romantic Gérard Philipe as Faust.

René Clair brought European style to Hollywood comedy, but in I Married a Witch, *his particular brand of fantasy became rather heavy (United Artists, 1942).*

A near-contemporary of René Clair was Jean Renoir, born in Paris in 1894. He was the younger son of the painter Auguste Renoir and inherited his father's eye for visual beauty and colour to set alongside his own flair for using music to express ideas – the two characteristics that lent a special magical glow to his best films. While Renoir believed, like Clair, that a person's fulfilment lay in understanding his or her naturally good nature, his approach to film-making was quite different, for Renoir concentrated on the individuality of his characters, observing them as closely as a portrait painter, though this sometimes works to the detriment of the action.

Boudu, the protagonist of *Boudu sauvé des Eaux* (*Boudu Saved From Drowning*, 1932) who is rescued from a watery grave in the Seine by a kindly bookseller, is a case in point. As played with unforgettable verve by Michel Simon, he was a real-life figure whom you would not be at all surprised to meet walking down the streets of Renoir's beautiful Paris, and as such, was as different as possible from Chaplin's archetypal Tramp. In Renoir's hands, Boudu is natural man, in contrast to the emasculated man of modern society that the bookseller, Lestingois, is seen to be. In the end, Boudu finds that life in the Lestingois household, where he has enjoyed the food and wine, *and* the wife and maid, is not for him, and he fakes a second drowning in the Seine, floating out safely out of sight before climbing out of the river to resume his old life.

La Règle du Jeu (The Rules of the Game) was Jean Renoir's view of the aimlessness and corruption of pre-war French society. Understandably unpopular when it was made, the film has come to be seen as Renoir's greatest work (Nouvelle Edition Française, 1939).

The theme, though in very different guise, underlies the much later Renoir film, *Le Carrosse d'Or* (*The Golden Coach*, 1953), in which Anna Magnani played an actress touring with a theatrical troupe in an impoverished South American country, where the ruling Spanish nobles live in isolated luxury in a palace that cocoons them from the reality of the poverty around them.

Renoir's greatest film, and also one of his most personal, was *La Règle du Jeu* (*The Rules of the Game*), a social comedy of manners that was a critical failure when it appeared in 1939, perhaps because in his subtle attack on the social code of his time, he was cutting too deeply, hitting too hard. Banned by the German occupation forces in France and its original negatives destroyed in a bombing raid, the film was pieced together again by loving hands in the 1950s. The 'game' in Renoir's film is life, especially life in a society where the only meaning is to be found in pleasure and diversion – in fact, the aimless, socially corrupt society of pre-war France – and the 'rules' of this game are those of the manners and morals – the social code – of the people who play it. Renior set his play in a château, ruled by the Marquis de la Chesnaye, played by Marcel Dalio, and various games are played in and outside the château by its aristocratic inhabitants and its servants. There is a wonderful farcical fête, a bloodily realistic hunting scene and a final tragic shooting, but throughout, Renoir's main preoccupation

In Jean Renoir's The Golden Coach *Anna Magnani was a passionate actress who rejected the fleshpots of Mexico to devote her life to her art* (Panaria-Hoche Productions, 1953).

The richly colourful world of the Moulin Rouge, probably experienced by Auguste Renoir, was lovingly recreated by his son, Jean Renoir, in French Can-Can *(Franco-London Films/Jolly Films, 1955).*

is with the reactions of his players to events and with the revelation of their essential character. Under the comedy, he is deeply pessimistic.

By the time of *French Can-Can* (also called *Only the French Can*, 1955), Renoir's mood and viewpoint had changed. In its colour and gaiety, this film looked not unlike one of his father's paintings and, set in the glittering Belle Epoque, showed Renoir's increased pre-occupation with the idea that art is, per-haps, more important than life, that in real life, the idea that natural man is good and only corrupted by civilization is too simplistic to explain the human condition.

Both Clair and Renoir were pioneers in film-making, experimenting with the new medium both for its own sake and to develop their own ideas through it. The other famous French film-maker of their period, Marcel Pagnol, born in Provence

in 1895, was rather different. He looked on films primarily as another way in which to increase the audiences for his plays. He was a writer/adapter and pro-ducer as well as a film director, with a splendid eye for good actors; it was Pag-nol who promoted the great talents of French stars Fernandel and Raimu.

The films most associated with Pagnol are the three based on his *Marius* trilogy, all set in the wonderfully colourful south-ern French world of Marseilles. *Marius* (1931), directed by Alexander Korda, set the scene and introduced the main char-acters, César , (played by Raimu) owner of the local bar, Marius his son (Pierre Fresnay) and Fanny (Orane Demazis), the owner of the local fishstall whom Marius loves — when he is not loving the sea more. *Fanny* (1932), directed by Marc Allégret, told what happened to Fanny when Marius disappeared to sea, leaving her pregnant with his child. She marries Panisse (Charpin), a rich sailmaker friend of César, but their peace is broken when Marius returns, claiming both Fanny and the child. *César* (1936) was directed by Pagnol himself, and carried the story on past the death of Panisse to a time when Fanny's son is now old enough to be told the truth about himself and his parentage. Together, the films were a delightfully warm pageant of the casual life of the port, with the atmosphere of the south of France and the Mediterranean wonderfully evoked.

Pagnol had to wait until the release of *La Femme du Boulanger* (*The Baker's Wife*, 1938) before his own talents as a director were recognized. This was an amusing tale of an unfaithful wife whose desertion so upset her husband that he refused to bake bread for the village. Everyone then had to find the errant wife to ensure a happy ending for all.

Pagnol's discovery, Fernandel, began his career in serious film roles before finding his *métier* in comedy movies. Once started in comedy, however, he soon became France's favourite funnyman, and was very popular in the rest of the Western world as well, especially in the United States and Britain, where his long, lugubrious face and toothy grin became as much a symbol of France as Gauloise cigarettes, black berets and accordion music played in the cafés of Montmartre. It

Above: Marcel Pagnol's trilogy of films about life in the French port of Marseille began with Marius, *the story of the unruly son of the café owner, César (Paramount/Marcel Pagnol, 1931).*

Left: The second in Pagnol's 'Marius' trilogy was Fanny, *in which the girl Fanny gave birth to Marius' son while he was away on his travels (Paramount/Marcel Pagnol, 1932).*

135

RAIMU
PIERRE FRESNAY
avec
CHARPIN
et
ORANE DEMAZIS dans

Un film de MARCEL PAGNOL

CÉSAR

avec MILLY MATHIS
E. DELMONT · ALIDA ROUFFE
PAUL DULLAC · VATTIER
DOUMEL · MAUPI
et
ANDRÉ FOUCHÉ

LES FILMS MARCEL PAGNOL · 13 Rue Fortuny. Paris

In César, *the last film in Marcel Pagnol's 'Marius' trilogy, Marius came home and all ended happily for the citizens of the port of Marseille (Paramount/Marcel Pagnol, 1936).*

was the small-town world of the priest Don Camillo, described first in 1952 in *Le Petit Monde de Don Camillo* (*The Little World of Don Camillo*) and then in a series of follow-ups, that brought Fernandel his international fame. He was the eccentric village priest, given to having private conversations with God in his church when he was not feuding with his friend Peppino, the town's Communist mayor. Fernandel was making the last Don Camillo film when he died of lung cancer in 1971.

Fernandel's place as the quintessential French comedian was filled to some extent by Jacques Tati, another long, gangling fellow, though he was never as popular in France as Fernandel. However unlike Fernandel, Tati was the complete film-maker, being writer and director as well as actor.

Tati, born in 1908, began his acting career as a musical-hall comedian in the 1930s, then went into films via comedy shorts, which were to become the seedbed for many comic sequences in his later feature films. Tati fans will know the final resting places of such short comic gags as *Oscar, Champion de Tennis* (1932), *On Demande une Brute* (*Brute Required*, 1934), and *L'Ecole des Facteurs* (*School for Postmen*, 1947), the last named of

which led directly to Tati's first feature film as a director, *Jour de Fête* (1949).

Tati was an original, and so was his great comic creation, Monsieur Hulot, even though Hulot's character as first seen in *Les Vacances de Monsieur Hulot* (*Monsieur Hulot's Holiday*, 1953) had a more than onomatopoeic resemblance to Charlot, as Chaplin was called in France. Hulot is a clown, he stalks about with a stiff-legged, uncoordinated gait, his clothes hang on him untidily and he always seems to be peering into some other world beyond the one inhabited by the people around him. In his holiday world, Monsieur Hulot is an oddball, regarded either with alarm or superiority by the other guests at his hotel except for a young boy and a very old man, both of whom are, like Hulot himself, outside the formal social structure of the world of the resort.

The Hulot character is not used by Tati to point a moral, even by implication, but by his ineptness, his obvious inability to fit in (though he is sublimely unaware of this), he makes the viewer question the behaviour of the 'normal' people. Hulot may look odd in his ill-fitting and dirty tennis clothes, but is his apparel any odder than those carefully ironed white trousers over which the young men have taken such pains? And is his weird tennis service any stranger than the careful stylishness of his opponents? At least his attempts to hit the ball are effective, because they are winners and because they upset the carefully arranged games of those who take their tennis seriously.

The great theme that ran through Tati's films – from his first feature, *Jour de Fête*, through *Mon Oncle* (*My Uncle*, 1958), *Playtime* (1968) and *Trafic* (*Traffic*, 1971) – was that of man versus machine, of people's inability to see that they have become trapped within the systems of the modern world, which they have built for themselves. In *Jour de Fête*, François the postman (Tati), inspired by a film about the speed and efficiency of the American postal system, tries to update his own bicycle-based delivery, but all ends happily when François gives up the unequal struggle and reverts to being the kind of postman who has time to stop and share a bottle of wine with his friends. *Mon Oncle* moved to the modern world of the city, where Hulot's brother-in-law has a house whose garage doors open apparently by themselves, where the ornamental trees in the garden are made of metal, where the kitchen stove turns itself on. Hulot cannot cope; he is a failure at all this sort of thing. *Trafic* has man battling with the motorcar (which Tati saw as an extention of man himself) and with the whole infrastructure of the automobile

Above: La Femme du Boulanger (*The Baker's Wife*) *was Marcel Pagnol's most successful and popular film (Marcel Pagnol, 1938).*

Left: Don Camillo (Fernandel) has a continuing ideological feud with the Communist mayor of the village (Gino Servi) but this does not prevent their being good friends; a scene from The Return of Don Camillo *(Francinex-Rizzoli/ Miracle Films, 1954).*

A sociable gathering of villagers enjoying the sun in Jacques Tati's Jour de Fête *(Francinex, 1949).*

business. Always, Tati's fine eye for the detail of how people behave, in different milieu and social situations, a subject which fascinated him, was put to hilarious use in these films.

None of the comedy film-makers so far discussed attacked established society with the quite the vim and venom of Spanish-born Luis Buñuel. Buñuel, born in 1900 and educated by Jesuit priests, became a friend of the surrealist left-wingers of the Spanish intelligentsia, and developed his ideas in the effervescent society of intellectual Paris. There, with his friend Salvador Dali, he made his first assault on the society of the post-First World War years with *Un Chien Andalou* (*An Andalusian Dog*, 1928), in which such notorious incidents as the cutting of a girl's eyeball with a razorblade and a hand (Dali's) being eaten by ants caused shock and revulsion. This short film, which with the passing of time has come to be regarded as a sort of black hole of

humour, was followed by the longer *L'Age d'Or* (*The Golden Age*, 1930), with its bitter attack on church and secular authority. Buñuel was unable, for financial and censorship reasons, to make films between 1932 and 1947, when he returned to the cinema screen with work that was unrelievedly tragic and powerful.

This extraordinarily complex and brilliant film-maker has a place in this book because of the deliciously witty and funny attack of such later works as *Le Charme discret de la Bourgeoisie* (*The Discreet Charm of the Bourgeoisie*, 1972), *Le Fantôme de la Liberté* (*The Phantom of Liberty*, 1974) and *Cet Obscur Objet du Désir* (*That Obscure Object of Desire*, 1977), which had been pre-figured by the comic-surrealist *El Angel Exterminador* (*The Exterminating Angel*), made in 1962 in Mexico where Buñuel lived for many years. Their basic theme was the hypocrisy of bourgeois attitudes towards most aspects of life, and were surrealist comedies of a compelling originality that ensured that they attracted a big audience wherever they were shown. The most entertaining of them is *Le Charme discret de la Bourgeoisie*, which concerns a group of friends whose attempts to have meals together are constantly thwarted by grotesque happenings that, since this is a surrealist comedy, are beyond reason.

While Buñuel was intent on assaulting the institutions of modern life, and depicted, through the lunatic behaviour of his characters, a whole world gone mad, we may suspect that his tongue was sometimes in his cheek, as in his personal anti-religious confession, when he said, 'thank God for my atheism.'

Italian cinema, like that of the French, knew early years of epic features interspersed with slapstick comedy shorts, though some fairly bland features of the early 1930s, such as Mario Camerini's *Gli Uomini che Mascalzoni!* (*What Rascals Men Are!*, 1932), hinted at what might be possible in a non-fascist world. Working with Camerini for a time was a young actor who would play a major part in the post-war renaissance of the Italian cinema – Vittorio de Sica — though at that time, the handsome young man was simply a popular matinée idol.

De Sica experienced personally the demoralization of the fascist years in Italy and the corruption and cynicism that followed. In him was the Italians' bitterness, but also their resilience of spirit and their ability to see the absurd in human behaviour, even in the worst of times. He had begun directing films during the war, his most notable film being the 1943 *I Bambini ci Guardano* (*The Children Are Watching Us*), a collaborative effort with the writer Cesare Zavattini. After the war, the two men joined forces again on two great films, in the style known as 'Italian neo-realism': *Sciuscià* (*Shoeshine*, 1946), and *Ladri di Biciclette* (*Bicycle Thieves*, 1948). The latter, in particular, was a brilliant film, a documentary-style story of life among the poor of Italy's cities, told with a compassionate warmth and deep conviction.

While *Bicycle Thieves* was not a comedy, except in the broadest sense that it was about the 'human comedy', De Sica's next film, *Miracolo a Milano* (*Miracle in Milan*, 1950), again scripted by Cesare Zavattini, did have considerable comedy in it. The story of a boy called Toto, living with the poor in a shanty-town outside Milan, his dead aunt appears out of the sky while he is climbing a flagpole and gives him a magic pigeon, which he loses. Meanwhile, oil is discovered underneath the shanty-town and the rich and powerful naturally come from Milan to drive

Monsieur Hulot (Jacques Tati) savouring the pleasures of the beach during his annual holiday, as hilariously depicted in Monsieur Hulot's Holiday *(Cady Films/Discina, 1953).*

20th Century Fox present   a Serge Silberman Production

Directed by Luis Bunuel

**The Discreet Charm
of the Bourgeoisie**

GREENWICH-FILM PRODUCTION

out the inhabitants and bulldoze down their shanties to get at it. The poor resist, and are bundled into police vans; as they are passing Milan cathedral, the pigeon comes back to Toto and, by magic, the vans fall apart and their occupants, pursued by the police, grab brooms from the street sweepers in the piazza and fly off into the sky ... or is it heaven?

Neo-realism in Italian films gave way to that period of critical self-examination in the 1950s and 1960s called *Il Ritratto Italiano*, during which all aspects of Italian life including the law, the church, politics and society were put under the microscope. It was a period that gave actors such as Ugo Tognazzi and Alberto Sordi the opportunity to project their special understanding of the Italian situation in their films.

Sordi, in particular, became one of Italy's most popular film personalities in the 1950s, playing in a wide range of mostly comedy films. He worked often with the director Dino Risi, not as well-known outside Italy as perhaps he should be, who combines an Anglo-Saxon style of blackish humour with the Italian *commedia dell'arte* tradition. The bitterness that lies at the core of much Italian comedy was shown in Risi's series of composite films comprising portraits of the 'new people' of the new Italy, the first of which was *I Mostri/Opiate '67* (15 from Rome, 1963).

Domestic life also received its share of attention during this period, most notably in De Sica's two delightful comedies starring Sophia Loren and Marcello Mastroianni, *Ieri, Oggi, Domani* (*Yesterday, Today, Tomorrow*, 1963) and *Matrimonio all'Italiana* (*Marriage Italian Style*, 1964). On both these films, the Neapolitan playwright Eduardo di Filippo collaborated on the screenplay with De Sica, who also came from Naples. Di Filippo's own typical Neapolitan warmth and humour, which help make his plays popular throughout the world, was apparent in the films he himself wrote and directed during the 1950s, though these are better known in Italy than abroad.

Another Italian director of the period who achieved more international prominence was Luigi Comencini, who produced a number of films with light-hearted, mass-market appeal, starting with the very successful *Pane, Amore e*

Fantasia (*Bread, Love and Dreams*, 1953), which starred Gina Lollobrigida and Vittorio de Sica. There were numerous films in the series, not all of them directed by Comencini, which looked in an amusing but sympathetic way at various aspects of Italian life, the most recent film being *Pane e Cioccolata* (*Bread and Chocolate*, 1973) directed by Franco Brusati, which investigated the problems of Europe's armies of migrant workers, in

Above: Sophia Loren and Marcello Mastroianni, in Marriage, Italian Style *(Paramount, 1964). Opposite: Julien Bertheau in* The Discreet Charm of the Bourgeoisie *(Greenwich Productions/Jet Film/Dean Film, 1972).*

141

Opposite: Ugo Tognazzi as the proprietor of a gay night-club and Michel Serrault as his drag artist friend, Zizi, strike typical poses in La Cage aux Folles II, *the follow-up to their international hit,* La Cage aux Folles *(United Artists/ Marcello Danon/ Artistes Associés, 1980).*

particular an Italian waiter (played by Nino Manfredi) working in Switzerland. He needs the job to provide for his family back in Italy; lose his job, and he would also lose his work permit and his right to stay in Switzerland. He leaves his position as a waiter in a smart restaurant (where the film offers some hilariously wicked views of the rich at table) to take a job with a rich ex-patriate Italian, but unfortunately the man dies, the waiter becomes unemployed and his troubles begin. ... The film is often farce, but the underlying tone is serious and a powerful attack on capitalist Europe.

The 1970s seemed to mark the end-point of the productive streams of French and Italian comedies of the previous decades. Since then, comedies have tended to be one-off affairs, like the delightful, glossy *Cousin, Cousine* (1975), about extra-marital relations, and *La Cage aux*

Folles (*Birds of a Feather*, 1978), which concerns two middle-aged gays who must at least appear to be going 'straight' because the son of one of them is about to marry into a respectable family. This was a very funny and finely observed French–Italian co-production, imaginatively directed by Edouard Molinaro, with Ugo Tognazzi as the father and Michel Serrault as his drag-artist friend.

For the moment, the initiative in the film comedy business seems to have passed firmly back to American and British film-makers, but this could be only a temporary state of affairs. As *La Cage aux Folles* demonstrated so happily, there is still plenty of comedy to be found in present-day Europe though, as in the United States, it is likely to be the comedy of personal expression and self-examination that we shall see, rather than comedy used as a weapon for social change.

Right: Gina Lollobrigida brings a caged bird and other problems to the chief of the village police (Vittorio de Sica) in Bread, Love and Dreams *(Titanus Productions, 1954).*

142

MODERN TIMES:
MOVIE COMEDY SINCE THE 1940s

While movie comedy production has been enormously prolific since the mid-Forties, when film studios and film-makers were able to shed their battle-dress and get on with making movies for a world that was more or less at peace, it has been a relatively small band of directors, writers and actors consistently producing the best films and the greatest performances.

The Second World War itself had not caused any slow-down of movie comedy production. On the contrary, comedy and musical comedy became major pre-occupations of the Hollywood studios, most of whose films, apart from semi-documentary and morale-boosting efforts, chose to ignore that the war was even happening. The view was that, in wartime, people wanted to escape from everyday worries and sadnesses – and audiences agreed.

A writer/director who enjoyed considerable popular success and critical acclaim during the war years, but sank more or less into oblivion not long after, was Preston Sturges. He had built up a good reputation as a writer of comedy films in the 1930s with films such as *Easy Living* (1937), and the Bob Hope/Martha Raye comedy *Never Say Die* (1939). When he returned to directing as well as writing, starting with the surprise hit of 1940, *The Great McGinty*, his style became urbane and sophisticated with a nicely satiric edge.

Brian Donlevy and Akim Tamiroff headed the cast of *The Great McGinty*, the story of a man on the skids (Donlevy) who wins the support of a crooked political boss (Tamiroff) by casting his vote 37 times for the same candidate in one day; when he tries to go straight, things go wrong. Sturges won an Oscar for his screen play.

After the first success, Sturges made some half dozen films during the war years, including such vintage comedies as *The Lady Eve* (1941) and *The Palm Beach Story* (1942).

One of the most popular providers of escapism during the war was the wisecracking, ski-nosed Paramount comic Bob Hope. After a few years in two-reel shorts and small parts in unremarkable feature films, neither of which suited the character of his comedy that had already been well-worked out during his early career in vaudeville, Hope was given the lead in that fine old war-horse of horror, *The Cat and the Canary* (1939). The film fitted him like a glove and had all the right ingredients: good story; lovely lady (Paulette Goddard); the perfect part to let Hope display his comedy *persona* of faint-hearted cowardice, tottering bravado and shining egotism; and plenty of room for the wisecracks and gags that have always been his hallmark ('Don't these big, empty houses scare you? a lady asks Hope. 'Not me,' he replies, 'I was in vaudeville.').

The film was a big hit, and Paramount quickly followed it with the similar *Ghost Breakers* (1940) and *Nothing but the Truth* (1941). In a way, Paramount were hedging their bets unnecessarily with these films, entertaining as they were, for Hope had struck another rich vein of comedy earlier in 1940 when he made the first of the 'Road' films, *Road to Singapore*, with the world's most popular crooner, Bing Crosby, and lovely, sarong-clad Dorothy Lamour. (Were Abbott and Costello trying to ride on her sarong hem with their 1942 *Pardon My Sarong?*) Hope, Crosby and Lamour were to make another six 'Road' films over the years, ending up in Hong Kong in 1962. The

Left: Preston Sturges' superb parody of American city politics, The Great McGinty, gave plum roles to Akim Tamiroff and Brian Donlevy (Paramount, 1940).

Below: Bob Hope trips the light fantastic to a musical accompaniment from Bing Crosby in Road to Singapore, *the first of the successful 'Road' series (Paramount, 1940).*

BING CROSBY
BOB HOPE
DOROTHY LAMOUR

ROAD TO MOROCCO

ANTHONY QUINN
DONA DRAKE
Directed by DAVID BUTLER

A PARAMOUNT PICTURE

The third of Hope and Crosby's 'Road' films, Road to Morocco, *saw the pair at their most spontaneous and relaxed (Paramount, 1942).*

best of this very popular partnership was seen, most people think, in *Road to Morocco* in 1942. This still looks a funny and delightfully spontaneous movie, reflecting its stars' relaxed attitude towards the business of being on the road together.

Bob Hope's best movies spanned about ten years, up to *Son of Paleface* (1952), and included, apart from some 'Road' films, *Monsieur Beaucaire* (1946), *My Favourite Brunette* (1947) and *The Paleface* (1948). He was usually partnered by one of Hollywood's more sexily beautiful women (e.g. Madeleine Carroll, Rhonda Fleming, Hedy Lamarr), the scripts were good, production values quite high and the general effect funny and fast. Later, as Bob Hope's radio and television careers became more and more successful, he seemed to lose interest in films, often choosing stories that did not quite suit him, or working with directors and writers who did not seem to know how to get the best from his talents. He was

perhaps lucky that his best days had coincided with Hollywood coming to terms with the peace and reassessing the nature of its audiences.

One of Hope's competitors in the 'Great Comics of the 1940s' stakes appeared in the unlikely shape of fastidious, correct Mr. Clifton Webb. He was an actor from an older generation, who had been out of the Hollywood scene for a long time until he made a noticeable comeback in the mid-Forties, being nominated for Academy Awards for his roles in two of the first (serious) films he made. In 1948 he took on the comic role of waspish, middle-aged babysitter Mr. Belvedere in the very funny hit *Sitting Pretty*, the one for which thousands cheered when the fed-up babysitter up-ended the bowl of porridge on his horrible charge's little head. There were several Mr. Belvedere sequels.

By this time, both Webb and Hope were competing with lesser fry and low-budget

146

Veteran Broadway actor Clifton Webb struck a successful movie vein in the late Forties with the character of Mr Belvedere; here, accompanied by Shirley Temple, Mr Belvedere Goes to College *(Twentieth Century-Fox, 1949).*

laughter fodder for the so-called 'family' audiences that the Hollywood bosses had decided were the great neglected area among cinema audiences. The years 1949 and 1950 saw the birth of two low-budget comedy series, designed for and, admittedly, highly successful with Saturday Matinée audiences: the 'Ma and Pa Kettle' series of nine films, starting off with *Ma and Pa Kettle* (1949) that was itself a spin-off from the successful tale of life down on the farm, *The Egg and I* (1947), starring Marjorie Main and Percy Kilbride as Ma and Pa; and the 'Francis' series. Francis was a talking mule, possessed of a much better mind than most of the humans around him, and the agreeable Donald O'Connor was his sidekick. The half-dozen Francis films were pretty banal, though pleasant enough, and the kids loved them.

1949 was also the debut year of a new and immediately very successful comedy team, Jerry Lewis and Dean Martin, in an indifferent comedy, *My Friend Irma*. Jerry Lewis was the comic and Dean Martin the straight man of the pair, and they already had several years of nightclub, cabaret and television success behind them. They were to star in seventeen movies, and to become the most popular showbiz duo in America, before splitting up amid arguments and recriminations in 1956.

Jerry Lewis is something of a puzzle among movie comics. Generally appreciated more in Europe, and especially France, than in his home country, his films, both with and without the easy-going Martin, have always seemed to most critics as something for the kids to laugh at uproariously rather than for mature grown-ups to sit through with any pleasure. But if this sounds as if his films have all been on the 'Ma and Pa Kettle' and 'Francis' level, that is to do them an injustice.

Part of Jerry Lewis's initial success lay in the fact that he looked funny. A skinny

lad with crewcut hair and a big, loose mouth, he looked a bit childishly simple, and he exaggerated this in his films with Martin, acting the complete clown and creating havoc and chaos with juvenile abandon. By the time he and Martin split up, Lewis had also grown up – or older. He could not go on playing the daft juvenile for ever. He was not too bad as a solo performer while he was being written for and directed by others, and with the experienced Frank Tashlin, in particular, he created some very funny and highly original gags in such films as *Rock-a-Bye Baby* and *The Geisha Boy* (both 1958) and *The Disorderly Orderly* (1964). But once launched really on his own, Jerry Lewis proved on the whole to be inadequate as a comic writer and as a director, and as an actor he tried too hard. You always felt with Lewis that it was all surface performance, with no underlying serious feelings about the roles he was supposed to be playing. Things were done for effect, not content, and his gags were worked out to look clever for their own sakes, not to be part of the continuity of the story. This was true with what is supposed to be his 'masterpiece', *The Nutty Professor* (1963), which he directed, produced, scripted and acted in. Its theme was Lewis's belief that everyone is two people, that we all have dual personalities, and his Professor Kelp's contribution to science was to devise a potion that would turn people into better, more confident versions of themselves. However, despite his failings, Jerry Lewis has been a successful comic performer for more than thirty years, with his recent excellent, serious performance in Martin Scorsese's brilliant and disturbing comedy–drama *The King of Comedy* (1982) suggesting a new turn in his career.

Two other comedians who found a firm place in Hollywood in the Forties and Fifties were Red Skelton and Danny Kaye. Red Skelton was the agreeable chap with

Virginia Mayo shows a keener interest in salesman Red Skelton than in his wares: a scene from The Fuller Brush Man *(Columbia, 1948).*

the funny, dimpled face, wide smile, red hair and freckles who provided the comic relief in such pleasant and enjoyable movies as *Bathing Beauty* (1944) and *Neptune's Daughter* (1949) – both of which were Esther Williams vehicles – *Three Little Words* (1950) and *Lovely to Look At* (1952). He was mostly a Metro-Goldwyn-Mayer player, which meant that that studio's particular brand of colourful, glossy, musical comedy was the territory within which he had to work, and in which his comic talents, which needed careful preparation and good direction, were not displayed to their best advantage. As comedians as notable as Buster Keaton and the Marx Brothers had discovered before him, it was not MGM's way to give comic actors their head, or to allow them enough independence to create movies that allowed their particular talents room to develop. Keaton, now a gag-man at MGM where he had once been a star, even suggested that he should be allowed to set up a unit within MGM especially to develop what he saw as Red Skelton's considerable comic abilities. But it was not to be, and Skelton's screen career was never as consistent or as successful as his later one on television, where he became a very big star indeed.

Still, Red Skelton managed to inject some very good and likeable comic scenes into many movies during his time in the ranks of Hollywood's laughter men. One of the best was the 'Guzzler Gin' routine he did for the MGM all-star, super-flossy *Ziegfeld Follies* (1946). In this, Skelton, set up before the camera without scenery and with few props, did his own special version of the comic's classic, the drunk scene. Other memorable pantomime bits can be seen in *Those Magnificent Men in Their Flying Machines* (1965).

Danny Kaye's career had its erratic ups and downs as far as the quality of his films went, but he himself was immensely likeable and very popular with cinema and stage/cabaret audiences for many years, particularly in Britain. His trademark, apart from his pleasing personality, was his vocal virtuosity, which first made its mark in a Broadway show called *Lady in the Dark* in which he did a patter number called 'Tchaikovsky' requiring him to reel off the names of fifty-four Russian composers (not all of them genuine) in thirty-eight seconds. Many of his best comedy songs were written for him by his wife Sylvia Fine.

Kaye's early films were made for Sam Goldwyn, who provided lavish colour, a beautiful blonde (usually Virginia Mayo), generally rather feeble scripts and stories, and plenty of opportunities for Danny Kaye to perform what were really cabaret acts inserted at intervals into the plot. Danny himself usually figured as the good but simple guy who makes it in the end in such films as *Wonder Man* (1945), *The Kid from Brooklyn* (1946), *The Secret Life of Walter Mitty* (1947), which was based, amusingly but remarkably, on the marvellous James Thurber short story, and *A Song Is Born* (1948).

After *Hans Christian Andersen* (1952), which had some attractive songs by Frank Loesser but not a lot else, Danny Kaye and his wife set up their own production company, hired some good directional and production talent and, among several films, came up with two classic movie comedies: *Knock on Wood* (1954) and *The Court Jester* (1956). In *Knock on Wood*, Danny was a cabaret ventriloquist who gets innocently mixed up with all sorts of shady international espionage agents, the climatic flight from whom involved him in a hilarious sequence amidst the cast of a ballet in performance. Mai Zetterling, the lovely blonde Swedish actress, had one of her few American film roles in this.

The Court Jester was the Danny Kaye film in which everything worked smoothly, including his tongue, which slipped neatly over such tonguetwisters as 'The pellet with the poison's in the chalice from the palace. The vessel with the pestle has the brew that is true.' A lot of money was spent on *The Court Jester* and it was used to good effect. Sets and costumes were lavish, if a little storybook stilted, the script sparkled, the comedy songs were good, and the whole thing was taken at a confident pace, allowing Kaye to display his gifts for mimicry, patter and good, old-fashioned pantomime to the full. There was even the splendid Basil Rathbone on hand to give the role of the villain real class and his sword-fight with Kaye plenty of finger-snapping zip.

Danny Kaye made another half-dozen films after this, including the attractive *Five Pennies* (1959), a biopic about jazz-man Red Nichols that had a memorable

SAMUEL
GOLDWYN
presents
DANNY
KAYE
VIRGINIA
MAYO

in The Secret Life of Walter Mitty *in* TECHNICOLOR

Released Through RKO Radio Pictures, Inc.

duet sung by Kaye and Louis Armstrong, but his life was mostly taken up with his work for UNICEF as well as the live stage and a highly successful television series, and he gradually disappeared from the Hollywood scene.

By this time, a new generation of movie comedians was beginning to establish itself, one of whose brightest stars was turning out to be Jack Lemmon. A serious actor who happens to have done his best work in comedy films, Lemmon came to Hollywood from the stage and television, and won an Oscar for Best Supporting Actor for his performance in his fourth movie, *Mister Roberts* (1955).

Since he won the Oscar for playing a naval ensign, a role he had already played in real life in the US navy, it might have just been a flash in the pan, but not so. Jack Lemmon has created so many perfectly judged roles – ranging from the side-splitting broad comedy of the musician

in drag in *Some Like It Hot* (1959), and the immoral black comedy of the upwardly mobile insurance company employee in *The Apartment* (1960) to the disillusioned garment manufacturer near the end of his tether in *Save the Tiger* (1973), for which he won an Oscar as Best Actor – that it is hard to pick out any one or two for special mention.

He had been particularly good in films by Billy Wilder – *Some Like It Hot, The Apartment, The Fortune Cookie* (*Meet Whiplash Willie* in UK, 1966), and *Avanti!* (1972) – and in two films based on the plays of Neil Simon, *The Odd Couple* (1968) and *The Prisoner of Second Avenue* (1975). His partnerships with Walter Matthau have produced some scenes to cherish, with big, bear-like, grumpy Matthau providing rich contrast with the leaner, hungrier-looking Lemmon – literally hungrier, too, in some of the funniest scenes in the very, very

Mad French hatter Anatole of Paris was one of several roles Danny Kaye created in The Secret Life of Walter Mitty, *from a James Thurber short story (RKO/Goldwyn, 1947).*

Josephine (Tony Curtis) and Daphne (Jack Lemmon) eyeing the Florida scenery rather apprehensively in Billy Wilder's Some Like It Hot *(United Artists, 1959).*

funny *Odd Couple*, about two divorced men setting up together in a New York apartment, in which Matthau's housekeeping, or lack of it (sandwiches going mouldy on the poker table, etc.), distresses the finicky Lemmon. Despite the fact that Matthau's part in *The Odd Couple* had been specially written for him to play on Broadway, Lemmon more than held his own in this one; he was, however, rather overshadowed by Matthau in *The Fortune Cookie*, which was hardly surprising since he spent much of the film laid low by an accident out of which Matthau, playing the part of his brother-in-law, spent much of the film trying to make monetary capital.

Matthau richly deserved his Best Supporting Actor Oscar for *The Fortune Cookie* and was nominated for an Oscar for his role in *Kotch* (1971), the first film to be directed by Jack Lemmon. Matthau had to age to a seventy-year-old for this comedy–drama about an irascible widower who can't live with his son and daughter-in-law – they are driving him crazy. It was a more than satisfactory directing debut for Lemmon, and another step for a good partnership.

Still, one can only be glad that Lemmon has not stayed behind the camera, since he has done plenty of good acting work since, including the politically serious *Missing* (1982), a powerful Costa-Gavras-directed movie about the political upheaval in Chile in 1973 that led to the overthrow of the Marxist Allende government. And if Lemmon had started out as a

Jack Lemmon and Walter Matthau in philosophical mood in the wonderfully funny movie version of Neil Simon's play The Odd Couple *(Paramount, 1968).*

director, then we would never have had such glorious moments of movie comedy as his tango, rose between the teeth, with Joe E. Brown in *Some Like It Hot*, or the scene in which, still dressed as Daphne and with maracas in hand, he announces to his partner in music and trouble, Joe/Josephine (Tony Curtis), 'I'm engaged, I'm engaged!' Indeed, his entire performance in that gem of a movie is something to be treasured.

If *The Odd Couple* marked just another step in the screen career of Jack Lemmon, for Walter Matthau it was a turning point. He had been moving between Broadway and Hollywood (where all they seemed to be offering were character parts) for some years before his role as the slob ex-husband in Neil Simon's *Odd Couple* made him an overnight sensation on Broadway. When the play had been filmed, Matthau was the man of the moment just about everywhere in the world where they watch American movies.

While Jack Lemmon may be seen as one of Hollywood's best actors, Walter Matthau must surely be one of Tinsel Town's best comedians, and throughout the Sixties and Seventies there were few to challenge him. Dustin Hoffman – despite his hilarious and touching performance in *The Graduate* (1967), Mike Nichols' brilliant depiction of a young man trying to come to terms with the values of his world, and Hoffman's even more brilliantly observed performance in *Tootsie* (1982) – is, like Lemmon, an actor first and a comic player second. George Segal has been attractive, engaging or just plain good in numerous movies, from the superb *Who's Afraid of Virginia Woolf* (1966), through the enjoyable romantic comedy *A Touch of Class* (1973) to the

College graduate Benjamin (Dustin Hoffman) receiving lessons in life and sex from Mrs Robinson (Anne Bancroft) in Mike Nichols' hilarious and hugely successful The Graduate *(Embassy/ Lawrence Turman, 1967).*

less funny comedy *Carbon Copy* (1981), but he always seems to be just a bit lightweight.

Dudley Moore – who achieved great success in the late Seventies and Eighties with *Ten* and *Arthur* (1981) – and Peter Sellers are part of a very select band of British comedy actors who have made it big in Hollywood. Sellers first made his mark, as far as the Hollywood moguls were concerned, in Stanley Kubrick's British-made *Dr Strangelove*, and they quickly put him into several Hollywood comic movies. The first of these was the best of what would become the six-film 'Pink Panther' series – *The Pink Panther* (1964), in which Sellers was crazy French detective Inspector Clouseau. Blake Edwards was the director of these hilarious movies.

The quality of the 'Pink Panther' series was variable and many people, it must be said, prefer the 1975 *The Pink Panther Strikes Again*, with its wildly funny slapstick, to the first one in the series. Sellers was also in *What's New, Pussycat?* (1965), the film that introduced Woody Allen to the world, as both writer and actor – a sort of modernized bedroom farce in which Peter O' Toole and Ursula Andress also figured prominently. In the seventies came *There's a Girl in My Soup* (1970) based on a popular West End and Broadway play, and *Murder by Death* (1976), a splendid parody by Neil Simon of a string of detectives from classic crime novels.

Seller's last film before his untimely death from a heart attack was the funny–sad *Being There* (1979), in which he

Peter Sellers created Inspector Clouseau for Blake Edwards' Pink Panther, *and repeated the part in several sequels.*

155

Peter Sellers as a zany psychiatrist in What's New, Pussycat?, *notable only for the fact that the film was Woody Allen's first screen appearance as actor and writer (United Artists/ Famous Artists, 1965).*

played a simple-minded gardener called Chance, whose gnomic utterances about gardening were taken to be of such prophetic political astuteness that they helped propel him to the White House.

Sellers' co-star in *There's a Girl in My Soup* had been the deliciously dizzy Goldie Hawn, making an early appearance in the screen career that would start fizzing in the late Seventies. She was delightfully kooky in the not always funny *Private Benjamin* (1980), fluttering those absurd false eyelashes above her army uniform, and good again with Burt Reynolds in the amusing *Best Friends* (1983), about the problems of holding on to the fine relationship that many couples have outside marriage, only to find that they are losing their grip on it within the bounds (or bonds?) or matrimony. There was more than a suggestion in these films that Goldie Hawn was not finding strong enough material to ensure her a permanent place among Hollywood's comparatively few recognized comediennes. She has still got plenty of time, though – and she's a blonde, which for some reason, seems to be a Hollywood prerequisite for a girl wanting lots of funny parts to play.

Lucille Ball was a red-head, of course, but she did have sparkling blue eyes, which lit up many a clowning scene with the likes of Red Skelton and Bob Hope in the Forties and Fifties. If anyone was, Lucille Ball was the female clown of immediately post-war Hollywood comedy, and she appeared in dozens of movies before becoming hugely successful as a

Peter Sellers and Goldie Hawn made a charming couple in the film version of the successful stage play, There's a Girl in My Soup *(Columbia/Ascot, 1970).*

Army life is clearly all too much of an effort for Goldie Hawn in Private Benjamin *(Warner Brothers/ Goldie Hawn-Nancy Meyers Productions, 1980).*

television comedy star in the Fifties – her television series *I Love Lucy* is still being re-run world-wide thirty years later.

Among Lucille Ball's best roles – and she did not have too many in films – were parts in films made in 1950. *Fancy Pants* had her starring with Bob Hope in a souped-up version of the Charles Laughton classic, *Ruggles of Red Gap*, with Hope in the Laughton role of the English gentleman's gentleman. The *Fuller Brush Girl* (*The Affairs of Sally* in UK) was perhaps an acknowledgment that Ball was Hollywood's female answer to the male clowns of Hope and Skelton, for she was actually playing the equivalent of Skelton's role in his slapstick hit of 1948, *The*

Fuller Brush Man. In her version, Lucille Ball was allowed to display her fine talent for slapstick to the full in a film script by Frank Tashlin.

Judy Holliday was a genuine blonde who played the type called 'dumb'. Her career was tragically cut short by cancer when she was only forty-three, but she made enough great films to ensure her Hollywood immortality. Her acting career took the unusual course, for she started out in Hollywood, first in a cabaret group and then in three minor films, going from there to Broadway and stardom in Garson Kanin's great comedy play *Born Yesterday*. She returned to Hollywood and to films, first of all to show

Tweedy Bob Hope coming to terms with the Wild West and its wild women – especially Lucille Ball – in Fancy Pants *(Paramount, 1950).*

those experienced and hardened performers Spencer Tracy and Katharine Hepburn how an exuberant blonde could steal scenes and almost an entire movie, in this case *Adam's Rib* (1949), from under their noses, and then to scoop the Oscar for Best Actress in 1950 – from under Bette Davis's nose – for her delicious performance in *Born Yesterday*. (The Davis role that got pipped at the post was, ironically, one of her best-remembered, that of the monstrous and marvellous actress Margo Channing in *All about Eve*, a superbly sophisticated and literate movie.)

In *Adam's Rib*, Judy Holliday played a bird-brained blonde suspected of murdering her husband. Hepburn was the lawyer defending her, Tracy the district attorney (and Hepburn's husband) prosecuting. She was Billie Dawn in *Born Yesterday*, the archetypal dumb blonde who turned out to be much shrewder than her boyfriend, Broderick Crawford – a millionaire junk dealer who, according to her, lacked 'couth'. She turned from him to William Holden for a crash course in culture.

Judy Holliday's later comedies, all marked by her intuitive sense of timing and bubbling exuberance, including the fast-moving *Phffft!* (1954), which had her teamed up beautifully with the relative new-comer Jack Lemmon in a story about a marriage that nearly went 'phffft', *The*

Right: Spencer Tracy and Katharine Hepburn played married lawyers on opposite sides of the court case in Adam's Rib; *Judy Holliday was the defendant in the middle (MGM, 1949).*

Opposite: Tom Ewell getting to know Marilyn Monroe, in The Seven Year Itch *(Twentieth Century-Fox, 1955).*

Below: That's the Encyclopedia Britannica that Judy Holliday is sitting on in Born Yesterday *while William Holden looks on (Columbia 1950).*

Solid Gold Cadillac (1956) and *Bells Are Ringing* (1960), one of Vincente Minnelli's finest adaptations of a Broadway musical. Judy starred as a telephone-answering-service operator, helping songwriter Dean Martin over a mental block. She was wonderful in it, which makes it all the more sad that it was her last movie before cancer caught her.

Marilyn Monroe, *the* blonde sex symbol of the day, also proved she could play comedy, when she was allowed to, giving memorable performances in *The Seven Year Itch* (1955), directed by Billy Wilder from the play by George Axelrod, and, of course, *Some Like It Hot*.

Then there was another blonde comedy star, Doris Day. No-one looking at her bright, shiny face, Pepsodent smile and bouncy blonde hair could have known that her life had been full of bad patches. Even her happy seventeen-year marriage to Marty Melcher ended in shock and horrified disappointment when she discovered after his death in 1968 that he had lost or embezzled away her entire $20 million fortune, earned over nearly a quarter of a century in show business and films. Doris had a nervous breakdown – then hit the top again as a television star, in a series her husband had set up for her before he died – that's show business . . . .

Doris Day helping
bring the Deadwood
Stage into town on
wings of song in
Calamity Jane
(Warner Brothers,
1953).

Doris Day's speciality was the romantic comedy, and her films became enormously popular, especially in the great heartland of middle America, whose movie-goers put her at the top of the list of the country's most popular female stars in the Fifties. She was also the most highly paid. At first, she played the tomboyish girl next door, starting off her films in pigtails then singing a song or two that were sure to reach the top of the Hit Parade, and fetching up in a pretty gown in time for the romantic kiss at the end, in such movies as *On Moonlight Bay* (1951), and *By the Light of The Silvery Moon* and *Calamity Jane* (both 1953). However, by the end of the Fifties, when they had begun filming her in soft focus, the films had become rather more apparently sophisticated in their attitude towards sex, though there was never any suggestion that Miss Day was other than a totally pure young lady. Her fans loved her in such movies as *Pillow Talk* (1959),

ROCK HUDSON · DORIS DAY "PILLOW TALK" IN EASTMAN COLOR CINEMASCOPE

CO-STARRING
TONY RANDALL
THELMA RITTER
WITH NICK ADAMS · MARCEL DALIO
JULIA MEADE
Directed by MICHAEL GORDON
Produced by ROSS HUNTER
and MARTIN MELCHER
Screenplay by STANLEY SHAPIRO
and MAURICE RICHLIN
AN ARWIN PRODUCTION
A UNIVERSAL Re-Release

Doris sings! Rock sings!
Your heart sings!
"PILLOW TALK" · "POSSESS ME"
"ROLY POLY" · "INSPIRATION"

That Touch of Mink (1962) and *Move Over, Darling* (1963), in which she starred with Rock Hudson and that sophisticated smoothie Cary Grant (still making stylish comedies, though *That Touch of Mink* – following *Houseboat* with Sophia Loren and *Indiscreet* with Ingrid Bergman, both released in 1958 – would be one of his last). These films allowed Day, like a Barbara Cartland of the movies, to carry single-handedly the light of old-fashioned romance into the permissive days of the 1960s, though it looked for a moment as if Jane Fonda, of all people, was going to be her successor. Her two pleasant romantic comedies of the Sixties, *Sunday in New York* (1964), and *Barefoot in the Park* (1967, from the play by Neil Simon – *again* – and co-starring Robert Redford), both had a touch of the 'cute' about them.

Apart from Doris Day, there was one other movie-maker who tried to stick with old-fashioned comedy. This was Stanley Kramer, who went all the way back to the slapstick world of Mack Sennett for *It's a Mad, Mad, Mad, Mad World* (1963), which he intended as a tribute to that great age of comedy and its stars. He assembled a huge all-star cast, lining them up behind Spencer Tracy and Mickey Rooney, spent a mad, mad, mad fortune and put his film on the wide screen. Although it had many funny gags and looked spectacular, the film did not work, mainly because, since it was on such a vast scale, with so many people, it would have been impossible to have recaptured the spontaneous, perfect insanity of the original slapstick world. At least Kramer was giving work to some very old hands, including Buster Keaton, Joe E. Brown,

Pillow Talk was a typical Doris Day vehicle, but one of the best, with deft performances from Rock Hudson and Tony Randall in particular (Universal/ Arwin Productions, 1959).

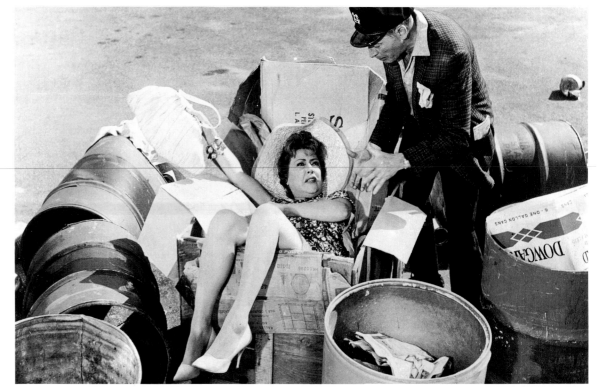

Milton Berle helping Ethel Merman out of a heap of trouble in Stanley Kramer's tribute to the great days of movie comedy, It's A Mad, Mad, Mad, Mad World *(United Artists/ Stanley Kramer, 1963).*

Beatrice Lillie has evil plans in a Chinese laundry for innocent Julie Andrews in Thoroughly Modern Millie, *but they come to nought (Universal, 1967).*

The Three Stooges, Ethel Merman, Milton Berle, Jimmy Durante, Buddy Hackett and Sid Caesar. It was to be the last film in a movie career stretching back to 1930, for 'Schnozzle-nose' Durante, though he would continue vigorously into the Seventies in nightclub acts and on television.

The time for old-fashioned comedy was past, and new styles were emerging in the more relaxed and permissive Sixties, with new writers, actors and directors to turn movie comedy into new directions.

George Roy Hill's *Thoroughly Modern Millie* (1967) was a particularly sparkling and entertaining showcase for a bevy of female talent. There were four of them – Julie Andrews and Mary Tyler Moore as a couple of Flappers, and Carol Channing and Beatrice Lillie, all doing their own thing to great effect in a musical comedy with a Twenties' setting. Bea Lillie, essentially a West End and Broadway star, who

had made her acting debut over fifty years before, provided the most memorable of only a handful of screen appearances, as a mad Chinese white slave trader. That other exuberant Broadway star, Carol Channing, had her third screen role in 'Millie', being nominated for a Best Supporting Actress Oscar for her performance.

People were even beginning to make comedies which included dead bodies, for goodness' sake, a much too tasteless subject for Miss Day's fans, many of whom had found it hard to come to terms with all the corpses in *Some Like It Hot*. The 'death comedy' of the mid-Sixties was Tony Richardson's *The Loved One* (1965), based on Evelyn Waugh's novel, which took an irreverent look at the funeral rites and customs of the people of California.

A few years later came the sleeper of the period, Hal Ashby's *Harold and Maude*,

Experienced actress Ruth Gordon was in fine form as wacky 79-year-old Maude inspiring love and devotion in a 20-year-old with a morbid interest in death, Harold (Bud Cort), in Harold and Maude *(Paramount/Mildred Lewis/Colin Higgins Productions, 1971).*

released to scant notice in 1971 but which became a cult movie of the highest order. *Harold and Maude* is a love story. Twenty-year-old Harold (Bud Cort), who derives peculiar enjoyment from faking suicides – even his mother (Vivian Pickles) hardly bats an eyelid when she finds him hanging from a chandelier – falls in love with seventy-nine-year-old Maude (Ruth Gordon), whom he meets at a funeral. The story of this unlikely romance is told with wry humour mixed with a wild lunacy interspersed with moments of pure lyricism. No wonder it's a cult movie.

The new directions of movie comedy had already been indicated by people such as Billy Wilder, maker of some of the most stylish and some of the blackest comedies ever to come out of Hollywood, and Woody Allen, chronicler of the neuroses of the New York male, sub-species Jewish, would be a major exponent of this trend. At first, Woody Allen looked as if he were going to be simply a funnyman, specializing in parodies. There was *What's Up, Tiger Lily?* (1966), for which Woody wrote the English-language soundtrack for an exceedingly silly but good-looking Japanese-made, James Bond-type thriller. The result was hilarious, with the Japanese hero, now renamed Phil Moskowitz, chasing after a stolen recipe for egg salad.

Allen then starred in, co-wrote and directed *Take the Money and Run* (1969), a joke about an incompetent crook (Allen, of course), and *Everything You Always Wanted to Know About Sex but Were Afraid to Ask* (1972), also with him as director, screenwriter and actor, was a series of episodes about sex, spoofing various kinds of film genres (including, hilariously, modern Italian movies) and with a cleverly done gag about sperm waiting to do the job for which they have been trained, in one orgasmic moment that will mean death for most of them. *Play It Again, Sam* (1972), based on Allen's own stage play, was more successful as a coherent piece of film-making. It was about a neurotic movie fan, abandoned by his wife and searching for another girl, who needed the constant psychological counselling of his idol, Humphrey Bogart. It was really an introductory piece about that New York-based male, full of neuroses, who would figure in the great Woody Allen movies of the late Seventies and Eighties.

Looking in other directions, there were signs that comedy was going to become more violent and bloodstained, mirroring, as had other movie genres, the violent times in which we live. In 1970, a year after Sam Peckinpah had released his extraordinarily bloody western, *The Wild Bunch*, there came *M*A*S*H*. It is doubtful if there will ever again be any comedy with opening scenes having the impact of those in *M*A*S*H*: this is an army medical unit in full swing on the edge of the Korean war zone, and there are bodies, like bleeding hunks of meat, all over the place, being put back together as best the medical staff can. There is also a lot of talk, from a lot of people: surely no one scripted the Babel of sound? Well, yes, Ring Lardner, Jr. did, and he won an Oscar for it. The brilliant direction was by Robert Altman, and the memorable performances came from, among others, Donald Sutherland, Elliott Gould and Sally Kellerman. *M*A*S*H* used its very considerable comedy and humour, not the blood and gore, to point out and satirize the brutalizing effects of war. It was comedy making serious statements about serious matters.

Waiting for the helicopter to bring in more wounded from the battle front in M*A*S*H (Twentieth Century-Fox, 1970)

THAT DISCREET
OBJECT OF DESIRE:
THE MOVIE COMEDY TODAY

Mathieu (Fernando Rey) is about as close as he is going to get to the desirable Conchita (Angela Molina) in Buñuel's That Obscure Object of Desire *(Greenwich Films/Les Films Galaxie/In Ciné, 1977).*

The desire of all writers, directors and actors of comedy is to cause their audience to see the humour of a situation. Sometimes the humour can be farcical, sometimes witty, sometimes satirical, and sometimes it is a black comedy that hovers on the edge of tragedy, and is only saved from becoming so by the absurdity of the way in which it is presented. This kind of black humour could be said to derive from Chekhovian drama in which characters, driven to the edge of insanity by their passions, are seen, in Russia at least, as figures of comedy.

In the contemporary world of film, two film-makers fit this concept of humour: one of them, Luis Buñuel, has reached the end of his life, and the other, Woody Allen, has moved from the humour of farce and situation to a reflective, self-searching film-making that hovers between comic fantasy and realism.

As we have seen, Luis Buñuel was a maverick in the world of cinema in the way that Picasso was in the world of art. In his last two films, he reaffirmed the content and style of the films that he had been making all his life, but in them, as he so often did throughout his life, he renewed himself and his work, creating among his critics a new confusion of interpretation and among his admirers a strengthening of their belief in his genius. Buñuel did not make things easy: unlike popular commercial film-makers, he did not tell you where the jokes were, nor even what the plot was, for to Buñuel, life remained a mystery to the end.

In *Le Fantôme de la Liberté* (1974), Buñuel starts his film with the execution of Spanish patriots in 1808. A captain of dragoons disinters a saint's body in perfect condition and takes her to his bedroom. Next, we are in a Parisian park in 1974, when a sinister figure approaches a nurse, a child and its parents and hands them some postcards, at the sight of which everyone looks shocked; the postcards merely show tourist sights. The film continues to develop along this line of contradictory images. Monsieur Foucauld, the father of the child, dreams that a postman delivers a letter that he has not

yet posted. A dentist's receptionist leaves to visit her sick father, but the road is blocked and she stays at an inn; in the inn are monks who play poker and pray for her father, an aunt having a *liaison amoureuse* with her nephew, another guest who invites them all to his bedroom to witness his flagellation. Next day a Monsieur Legendre goes to the police station to report the disappearance of his daughter, who is with him and describes herself to the police. Meanwhile, a sniper picks off people in the street, and a police chief gets a phone call from his dead sister. Going to the vault in which she was interred, he finds no one there, and he is arrested for desecration of the tomb and taken to the zoo by the police chief to stop a riot. The film ends with an ostrich staring at the camera.

What was Buñuel trying to tell us in these absurd, surrealist images that move so naturally, if disjointedly, from one to the other? Is it that we are always deceiving ourselves, seeing only what we want to see or, like the ostrich, hiding our heads in the sand?

In his last film, *Cet Obscur Objet du Désir* (*That Obscure Object of Desire*, 1977), Buñuel drove the point home brilliantly. Mathieu (Fernando Rey) fancies Conchita (played by two women, Carole Bousanet and Angela Molina) who has been engaged by his butler. He eyes her, she disappears. He meets her again in Switzerland where she wants to borrow money to visit her mother in Paris. Mathieu meets the mother and comes to a financial arrangement over Conchita who promptly disappears again. She does not want to be bought, but later she agrees to live with him. He is allowed only to caress her, but then finds her apparently intimate with a guitar player. Conniving with his friend, the magistrate, he has Conchita deported to Spain and later meets her in

Luis Buñuel seldom missed an opportunity to shock the religious, as in the opening scenes of Le Fantôme de la Liberté *(Greenwich Films/ Serge Silberman Productions, 1974).*

That's Woody Allen suffering for his art in Sleeper. *Diane Keaton is in attendance (United Artists/Jack Rollins-Charles H. Joffe Productions, 1973).*

Seville where she dances nude for tourists. He buys her a house and she tells him she is still a virgin, so he beats her. As he gets on the train to leave her, she appears and he throws a bucket of water over her. Later, on the train, she does the same to him. They get off the train in Paris together and are seen walking along a street when a bomb explodes, filling the screen with obscuring smoke and dust.

Once again, the audience is left wondering what the obscure object of desire is. Perhaps it is the unattainable fulfilment and truth that constantly eludes us, and that will always elude us to the end, the object that we will do anything to attain, even resorting to terrorism. Whatever it is, Buñuel leaves the answer hanging in the outer space of the mind, kept aloft like a ping-pong ball in a fairground shooting gallery by the air jets of his brilliant, surrealist, black comedy images.

Unanswered questions have also been a characteristic of the work of Woody Allen in the past decade, during which he has moved from the slapstick-cum-Monty Python style of the *Everything You*

Always Wanted to Know About Sex but Were Afraid to Ask routines into self-searching comedies of an intensely personal nature.

The change in direction began with *Annie Hall* (1977) – which won Academy Awards for Best Picture, Best Direction, Best Screenplay and, for Allen's co-star Diane Keaton, Best Actress – and turned to serious, even tragic themes with no comedy of any kind in *Interiors* (1978). In *Annie Hall*, a forty-year-old New Yorker looked back on his life, his hopes for the future and his relationships with women: 'Even as a kid, I always went for the wrong woman. I feel that's my problem. When my mother took me to see *Snow White*, everyone fell in love with Snow White. I immediately fell for the wicked queen.'

With *Manhattan* (1979), in which Woody Allen the actor played Isaac Davis, a successful writer of television comedies, Woody Allen the director was emphasizing place and characterization rather than comedy. Isaac is having an affair with Tracy (Mariel Hemingway), which makes him insecure because she is so much younger than he is; he also is anxious because his ex-wife Jill (Meryl Streep) is writing an exposé of their marriage. Isaac gives up his television career to write a serious book, and then meets Mary Wilke (Diane Keaton), the girlfriend of his best friend Yale. Yale gives her up but she tells Isaac that she still loves him; Isaac discovers that he still loves Tracy but she is off to London and tells him to wait for her.

The story could almost be that of a downmarket novel but for the cool, ironic style in which it is told. Manhattan – filmed in glorious black-and-white – and its self-absorbed people are the subject, with the city being very much part of the film. As in his next film *Stardust Memories* (1980), in which Allen is a successful film-maker besieged by girls and sycophants, Woody Allen in *Manhattan* is preoccupied with the purpose, or lack of it, of human activity, unlike Buñuel who was preoccupied with existence itself. In particular, Allen is concerned about artistic endeavour – is art a pretension, a disguise, an escape? Diane Keaton says early in *Manhattan* that there is an academy of over-rated talent – Gustav Mahler, Heinrich Böll, F. Scott Fitzgerald are members.

Annie (Diane Keaton) and Alvie Singer (Woody Allen) pursuing an acquaintance begun on the tennis court in Annie Hall *(United Artists/Jack Rollins-Charles H. Joffe Productions, 1977).*

171

Above: Woody Allen and Mia Farrow enjoying a Bergmanesque country idyll in A Midsummer Night's Sex Comedy *(Orion/Jack Rollins-Charles H. Joffe Productions, 1982).*

Right: Danny Rose (Woody Allen) and Lina Vitale (Mia Farrow) have chosen the sidewalk as the place for a major row in Broadway Danny Rose *(Orion/Jack Rollins-Charles H. Joffe Productions, 1984).*

Woody Allen has continued to change the viewpoints of his movies. *A Midsummer Night's Sex Comedy* (1982) was a witty and delicate mingling of sex and comedy with a distinctly Ingmar Bergman flavour, with Mia Farrow playing the female interest. *Zelig* (1983) was splendidly inventive in its parodying of numerous movie forms, including those portentous 1930s and 1940s newsreels, even as it was telling the story of the amazing Mr. Leonard Zelig, the so-called 'Chameleon Man', a nonentity born with the involuntary ability to turn into any person with whom he associated, be they black or white, democrat or fascist, cowboy or baseball player. This time, Mia Farrow was Zelig's psychiatrist. In *Broadway Danny Rose* (1984), Woody Allen played the title role, once a not very good stand-up comic and now an artists' agent with a distinctly odd list of clients, one of whom gets mixed up with a blonde (Mia Farrow)

and her Mafia connections. Danny himself seems less neurotic, more accepting of life than Woody Allen's earlier characters, so perhaps there is a change of direction here too. In 1985 he won a 'Stella' award from the British Academy of Film and Television Arts (BAFTA) for the screenplay of *Broadway Danny Rose*, but although nominated for an Oscar in the same category, he lost to Robert Benton for *Places in the Heart*.

Woody Allen's is a narrower and more tangible cosmos than that of Buñuel but its tensions are not entirely dissimilar, and if the humour, created by a man who is now a master of his craft, does not provoke hearty laughter, at least it stays with you a long time.

Buñuel and Allen, representing the deeper levels of humour and a continuity of thought in their film-making, have few equals, though Miloš Forman's *One Flew Over the Cuckoo's Nest* (1975) can be said

Jack Nicholson proving a disturbing influence among his fellow patients in Miloš Forman's One Flew Over the Cuckoo's Nest *(United Artists/Fantasy Films, 1975).*

Airplane II: The Sequel *left Earth behind completely, but its trip to the moon could not sustain the same amount of laughter that* Airplane *had generated (Paramount, 1982).*

to be in the same line of comedy. Czech-born Forman, who lost both his parents to Nazi concentration camps, first made his mark in America with the amusing *Taking Off* (1971), in which parents try to understand their children by emulating them, but it was *One Flew Over the Cuckoo's Nest* – which won Academy Awards for Best Picture, Director, Screenplay, Actor and Actress – that established him firmly as one of the great contemporary directors. In this Jack Nicholson was Randel Murphy, a cheerful but anarchic character consigned to a mental hospital where he inspired the patients to rebel against the strait jacket of the established bureaucracy headed by Nurse Ratched (Louise Fletcher). His refusal to conform found

expression in a number of humorous incidents, the final one being a party held in the ward with liquor smuggled in by two of Randel's girlfriends. This extreme example of insubordination condemned Randel to a lobotomy and drove his Indian friend, Chief Browden, to smother him with a pillow before escaping himself. The end was tragic, but the events leading up to it were treated with the sure touch of a man who knows that human crassness can have its funny side even though it can lead to disaster.

Forman's latest film, *Amadeus* (1984), was based on a successful stage play by Peter Shaffer, in which respected, hard-working and worthy musician Antonio Salieri (F. Murray Abraham, who won one of *Amadeus*'s eight Oscars) is goaded into murder by the fact that a scapegrace, foul-mouthed joker called Wolfgang Amadeus Mozart (Tom Hulce) writes infinitely finer music than he does. Ironically, only Salieri among his contemporaries recognizes Mozart's genius. Forman has created yet another memorable and thought-provoking film, in which the racy pace of the story is set against an elegant 18th-century Vienna (actually Prague).

If the directors so far discussed have been producing comedy for a perhaps more intellectually keen audience, there has been plenty going on for audiences who want comedy on a lighter level. The spoof comedy, lampooning to hilarious effect various film genres, has been a highlight of the past decade or so of Hollywood film comedy.

There was, for instance, *Airplane* (1980), a gag-laden spoof of the disaster series that began with *Airport* (1970) and ended three films later with *Airport '79 Concorde*; the spoof was so successful that a follow-on, *Airplane II* (1982) was called for. *Top Secret* (1983), a more recent exercise in the spoof movie, now almost a genre in itself, was a take-off of spy movies and involved a young and astonishingly naïve pop singer on tour on the wrong side of the Berlin Wall, who becomes involved in all sorts of spying shenanigans, including the crushing of incompetent spy Omar Sharif in a car in a breaker's yard so that spy and car become one, strangely human, talking, eye-blinking piece of machinery.

Foremost director, producer and writer of the spoof comedy has been Mel Brooks,

Top Secret, *a mid-Eighties spy spoof, managed a few surrealist moments among the rather juvenile belly laughs (Paramount, 1983).*

Above: Despite many bad notices for its tasteless lack of wit, unfunny jokes, etc, Mel Brooks' The Producers has become a cult movie (Avco Embassy/Sidney Glazier Productions, 1967).

Right: Mel Brooks casts a directorial eye over a fine cleavage in his spoof western, Blazing Saddles (Warner/Crossbow, 1974).

176

whose films, stretching from the late 1960s to the present, have combined laughter and awful bad taste in cheerful abundance.

The Producers (1967), which Brooks wrote and directed, winning the Best Screen Play Oscar for his efforts, contained the ultimate in brilliant bad taste – a jolly swastika-draped dance number for a Broadway show called 'Springtime for Hitler'. That great stage and screen character actor, Zero Mostel, played a down-and-out Broadway producer looking for a quick million, and Gene Wilder was his accountant/assistant, giving a performance that won him an Oscar nomination.

Blazing Saddles (1974) was a western like no other before it. It was the story of a black sheriff (Cleavon Little) trying to bring law and order to Rock Ridge who was successful enough to cause the villain who had ordered him there – hoping to create enough chaos so that the place

would be easy pickings – to send in the army to get it back. The townspeople build a fake Rock Ridge, which the army blows up, precipitating the cast of *Blazing Saddles* into the set of the musical extravaganza being filmed next door, a gag that had been used more than a generation before in *Hellzapoppin'*.

Mel Brooks followed this chaotic farce with *Young Frankenstein* (1974), a horror movie spoof, with Gene Wilder, who had played in *Blazing Saddles*, as the young American brain surgeon Frederick Frankenstein, who is also the grandson of the notorious Dr. Frankenstein. Also in this was another of the *Blazing Saddles* cast, the rising young comedy actress Madeline Kahn. *Young Frankenstein* was filmed in black and white and managed to look splendidly like all those spine-chillers of the 1930s. It had some marvellously mad moments, like the scene in which young Dr. Frankenstein, back in America with

Glamorous Madeleine Kahn has an admiring look for Gene Wilder, playing the young American member of the Frankenstein family who has inherited the family castle, and more besides, in Transylvania: Mel Brooks' spoof spine-chiller, Young Frankenstein *(Twentieth Century-Fox/Gruskoff/ Venture Films/Jouer/ Crossbow Productions, 1974).*

If the past decade in Hollywood has been characterized on one level by the spoof comedy, it has also produced a whole clutch of movies whose comedy has been drawn from the source of all comedy – real life, in all its wonderful, mad variations.

Having made the slapstick-style *What's Up, Doc?* with Barbra Streisand in splendid clowning form and Ryan O'Neal in 1972 as his own homage to the screwball comedies of the Thirties, the director Peter Bogdanovich put Ryan O'Neal and his daughter Tatum into *Paper Moon* (1973), a sentimental view of rural America *à la* John Ford. Ryan was Moses Pray, a Bible-selling con-man operating in the poor American cornbelt in the 1930s and Tatum was the child Addie, with whom Pray (who may or may not be her father) gets saddled after her mother is killed in an automobile accident. He is supposed to be taking her to her aunt in Missouri, and their adventures across America makes an amusing and warmhearted story, despite Moses Pray's dishonest ways. Addie, of course, always gets the better of him, and much of the comedy arises from her cheeky toughness (for which Tatum O'Neal won an Oscar) contrasted with his constant discomforture.

While this film was a big success for Bogdanovich, his comedy about the days of the silent movie, *Nickelodeon* (1976), was torn to pieces by the critics, as had been the two films of his that had preceded it, and more recent work has fared little better.

A director who has been much more successful in recent years has been John Landis, who in 1978 came up with the low comedy *National Lampoon's Animal House* starring John Belushi from American television's *Saturday Night Live*, followed that with the off-beat horror-comedy, *An American Werewolf in London* (1981), and then hit the jackpot with *Trading Places* (1983). Other veterans of *Saturday Night Live*, the white Dan Aykroyd and black Eddie Murphy had starring roles in this, the latter having already given a show-stealing performance the year before as a con-man temporarily released from prison to help in the capture of an escaped convict in Walter Hill's breathless and anarchic *Forty-eight Hours*. Also in the splendid cast of *Trading Places* were two survivors from the

Above: Ryan O'Neal looks as if he cannot take much more in What's Up, Doc?; *Barbra Streisand is more optimistic (Warner/Saticoy Production, 1972).*

Opposite: Ryan and Tatum O'Neal in Paper Moon *(Directors Company/ Saticoy Production, 1973).*

his own newly-built monster (Peter Boyle), dons top hat and tails to give a dancing demonstration of how sweet and tractable – *and* alive – his creation is.

After this came *Silent Movie* (1976), literally a silent movie in which the best joke came with the film's one sounded word spoken by the famous French mime actor Marcel Marceau; *High Anxiety* (1977), a take-off of a number of Hitchcock films; *To Be or Not to Be* (1983), a re-run of the Ernst Lubitsch classic and a black comedy about an egotistical actor–manager (Brooks) working in Nazi-occupied Warsaw.

John Landis first showed his film directorial talents in the very basic comedy of National Lampoon's Animal House *(Universal/Matty Simmons-Ivan Reitman, 1978).*

good old days of Hollywood, Ralph Bellamy and Don Ameche, as well as English actor Denholm Elliott, who seems to have struck a new rich vein of talent in a series of character roles in recent years.

Trading Places took the lid off the world of the American commodities markets, while offering a hilarious and cynical slice of New York life in a tale about what happens when prissy stockbroker Winthrop Duke (Aykroyd) is tricked into gutter-level poverty, while a petty New York conman, Valentine (Eddie Murphy), is installed in his place – complete with luxurious house with live-in valet (Elliott), well-tailored suits, Mercedes and so on – by Winthrop's two conniving old uncles (Ameche and Bellamy), who set up their

dastardly deed for a mere $1.00 bet.

Only a year after this, Eddie Murphy came up with another great performance, this time as a wickedly charming and clever policeman in *Beverly Hills Cop*, a film that was set to gross over $100 million in US domestic rentals within a few months of its release. Eddie Murphy is clearly one of the new superstars of American movies – and deservedly so, on his present showing.

An older superstar also hit the top in another sort of 'trading places' comedy in the early Eighties. This was Dustin Hoffman, who put himself into brilliant drag for *Tootsie* (1982). For many people, this was the funniest and most stylish comedy to come out of Hollywood since *Some*

Their disguises penetrated by the villain they are stalking, Dan Aykroyd, Jamie Lee Curtis, Eddie Murphy and Denholm Elliot are having to do some quick thinking in Trading Places *(Paramount/Aaron Russo Production/ Landis-Folsey, 1983).*

Above: Sydney
Pollack, actors' agent,
and behind the
feminine trappings,
Dustin Hoffman in a
scene from Tootsie
(Columbia/Mirage
Enterprises/Punch
Productions/Delphi/
Black Rhino, 1982).

Opposite: Eddie
Murphy in Beverly
Hills Cop
(Paramount/Don
Simpson/Jerry
Bruckheimer/Eddie
Murphy Productions,
1984).

Like It Hot, and while this may be a bit of
an exaggeration, it is true to say that
Hoffman, squeezed into bra, girdle and
dresses, was very good indeed in this
sensitively handled exploration of sexual
role-playing.

Tootsie is the story of an out-of-work
actor Michael Dorsey (Dustin Hoffman)
who, partly in a spirit of sardonic rebel-
lion, but also because he needs the job,
dresses himself up as a female actress
whom he calls Dorothy Michaels and
auditions for a role in a television soap
opera called 'South-west General'. Dorothy gets the part and becomes enormously popular; she also becomes good
friends with another actress, Julie (Jessica
Lange), with whom Michael, under all

that terrific make-up, falls in love. As an
added complication, Julie's father
becomes extremely attracted to Dorothy
... In the background is Michael/Dor-
othy's increasingly nervous agent, played
by Sydney Pollack, who also directed the
film. In the end, the tension becomes too
much for Dorothy and she tears off her
wig and glasses and confesses all on
nationwide television. Since the film is a
comedy aiming at a wide market, Dorothy
is not lynched, and all turns out for the
best in the end.

Tootsie's director, Sydney Pollack, had
a number of good films behind him when
he made this one, and is one Hollywood
director of whom more may be expected
in the future. Henry Jaglom, despite two

fine comedies to his credit, is much less well known, but it is none the less worth watching for all that. One day, his *Sitting Ducks* will surely be recognized as a great comic movie by more than just film buffs and a few film-makers such as Scotland's Bill Forsyth. Released in 1979, this is an anarchic tale of two petty criminals (Michael Emil and Zack Norman) who manage to steal a fortune and head south to Florida where, on a remote beach, they expect an aeroplane to lift them and their money to safety and comfort in Costa Rica. They pick up a couple of girls on the way, and the story of the foursome's antics and adventures in their car, just a few steps ahead of the mobsters pursuing them, is both slapstick and raunchy, but also oddly appealing.

Henry Jaglom put Michael Emil, who just happens to be his brother, in his next comedy, *Can She Bake a Cherry Pie?*

(1983), a romantic comedy that begins when two people meet in a café in New York. The man, comfortably middle-aged Eli (Michael Emil), is a super-talker, and the woman is Zee (Karen Black), a singer whose husband has just walked out on her. Henry Jaglom's account of Eli's pursuit of Zee is lightly, unsentimentally told with some delightfully funny and absurd detail of these middle-aged New Yorkers working out their relationship. Jaglom is definitely a director to watch out for.

Films like these indicate that there is plenty of life in the basic American comedy film, and an abundance of talent to put it on the screen. Across the Atlantic, British films such as *Educating Rita* (1984), starring Michael Caine and Julie Walters (who won a British Academy Award for this) and directed by old-hand Lewis Gilbert, and the fine comedy of Bill Forsyth suggest that here, too, is another

Zee (Karen Black) and Eli (Michael Emil) met in a New York café in Can She Bake a Cherry Pie? *(International Rainbow Pictures/ Jagfilm, 1984).*

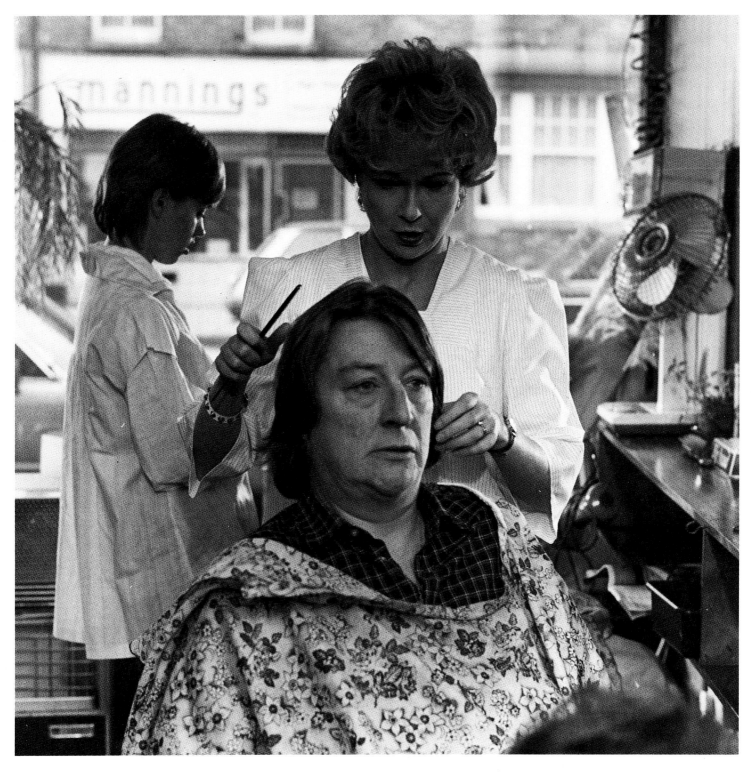

source of good, genuinely funny, well-made movies.

But if there is life in the basic American movie comedy, what is the direction being indicated by such recent films as *Gremlins* and *Ghostbusters* (both 1984). These two have been decribed as comedies, and their appeal was originally and essentially for the kids' market. *Gremlins*, a comic-horror film with the laughs coming from the antics of monsters rather than people, is in the Steven Spielberg *ET* tradition, with a mysterious cuddly creature turning up in smalltown America and, once accepted,

producing a whole horde of lookalikes that proceed to wreck the community: the ghastly cuteness of *ET* has gone out of the window, but whether this is for good remains to be seen – and for Steven Spielberg to decide.

Ghostbusters was meant to be a romp, with a myriad jokey, half-scary effects as well as a topping of low humour of the kind exhibited in John Landis's *National Lampoon's Animal House*, and it succeeded to such effect that it, and *Indiana Jones and the Temple of Doom* (released in the same year), established a new

Julie Walters, a hairdresser and mature university student tends to a difficult client in Educating Rita *(Lewis Gilbert Films/Acorn Pictures, 1984).*

185

On the trail of the supernatural in the streets of New York: the Ghostbusters *step out (Columbia/Bernie Brillstein Productions, 1984).*

STEVE MARTIN · LILY TOMLIN

ALL OF ME

The comedy that proves that one's a crowd.

Steve Martin and Lily Tomlin in Carl Reiner's excellent All Of Me *(Universal/Kings Road/Stephen Friedman Productions, 1984).*

money-making record for the American domestic market. It was the first time that two films took over $100 million each in domestic rentals in one year.

Ghostbusters, directed by Ivan Reitman, was lucky in its cast, which included the nicely contrasting Bill Murray as a slob, a very correct Dan Aykroyd and intellectual Harold Ramis, all trying to free New York of a plague of poltergeists. Unfortunately, they get mixed up with a Sumerian demi-god on the way ... The

kids, scared stiff for some of the time, loved *Ghostbusters* for most of the time.

Hollywood calculates that its cinema-going public comes very largely from the fourteen to twenty-five-year age group, whose big loves are action-adventure movies, comedy and something that has been derisively called 'tits and ass' movies, these being catered for by the *Porky* kind of film. This still leaves a big potential audience for some real comedy, so it is safe to assume that the movie comedy will continue to be a Hollywood pre-occupation. The town has got the talent – not as much as it had in the Thirties, perhaps, when the pool of acting, directing, writing and producing talent seemed bottomless, but still plenty.

Gene Wilder, star of many Mel Brooks movies, had his own hit with *The Woman in Red* in 1984; actor-turned-director Ron Howard had considerable success with *Splash*; Steve Martin, who appeared with Lily Tomlin in *All of Me*, scooped a New York Critics Best Actor of the Year award for his performance; Bill Murray and Eddie Murphy were both voted into the Top Ten in a major box-office survey; and Dudley Moore garnered many more-than-kind critiques for his performance in *Micki and Maude* late in 1984 .... The list could go on and on.

And of course, there is the never-failing Woody Allen. Even while his *Broadway Danny Rose* was waiting for the 1984 Oscar results, he was seeing his next film, *The Purple Rose of Cairo*, into the 1985 Cannes Film Festival.

Dudley Moore in double trouble with a wife (Amy Irving and Ann Reinking) on each arm in Blake Edwards' Micki and Maude *(Columbia, 1984).*

INDEX

190